FIRST FORM LATIN

Teacher Manual

Cheryl Lowe

MEMORIA PRESS
www.MemoriaPress.com

FIRST FORM LATIN

TEACHER MANUAL
Cheryl Lowe

ISBN 978-1-61538-001-5

First Edition © 2009 Memoria Press 0417

TABLE OF CONTENTS

First Form Latin

Teaching Guidelines

TEACHING GUIDELINES

Introduction

First Form is designed for teachers with or without a Latin background. The *First Form* series will cover all of the Latin grammar in four texts: *First, Second, Third,* and *Fourth, Forms.* Each text is designed to be a small book of approximately 100 pages with 30-35 concise two-page lessons. Each lesson is organized on facing pages and contains a Latin Saying, a set of grammar forms, vocabulary, grammar lessons, and elementary syntax.

Each text has a corresponding workbook with 4-6 pages of exercises per lesson. The exercises guide the student and teacher through the lesson. The workbook provides both the novice and the experienced teacher with well-designed drills and exercises that ensure mastery learning. Weekly quizzes, cumulative tests, flashcards, an audio, and DVD provide the teacher or homeschooler with everything needed to be successful.

If you are a teacher or homeschooler without any Latin background, a Latin text can be very intimidating. However, you *can* learn Latin and teach your children or students at the same time if you are patient, calm, and let the workbook guide you through the lesson.

If you are an experienced Latin teacher I hope this program helps you to be a more effective teacher. I hope your students learn Latin more thoroughly and with more pleasure using the *First Form* Series. Mastery is the key to success in Latin. Students enjoy what they have thoroughly learned. They do not enjoy what they have half-learned and half-understood.

The focus of the *First Form* series is the Latin grammar and a small, usable, vocabulary. Translation and syntax are kept to a minimum and are for the purpose of vocabulary and grammar drills. Translation and syntax are *logic* and *rhetoric* level skills. Beginners, regardless of age, are not at that level. The beginner is quite overwhelmed with the whole newness of Latin and the demands that it makes on the memory. The beginner should be allowed to focus on the grammar without the distraction of the many little details of syntax and the time required to learn and apply them in translation.

There are some who believe that the memorization part of Latin is boring and causes students to lose interest in Latin, but I disagree. I think it is the adults who find it boring <u>and</u> difficult, not the students.

Below is what I consider to be an ideal Latin scope and sequence. It is based on the trivium—the grammar, logic, and rhetoric stages of learning. These stages apply to all learners, regardless of age.

Grades 3-6	Grammar stage. Memorize the Latin grammar and a limited vocabulary. (400 - 800 words)
Grades 6-8	Logic stage. Master syntax and translation skills and continue building vocabulary. Translation: music and prayers in *Lingua Angelica*; selections from the gospel of Mark; exercises in *Henle I* and *II.*
Grades 8-12	Rhetoric stage. Latin literature: Ovid, Caesar, Cicero, Catullus, Horace, Vergil, St. Augustine, Aquinas.

It's never too late to learn Latin. Do not be concerned if you are beginning Latin and your child or your students are older than the 3rd grade. Older students can cover the First Form series in less time than elementary students. So any age is a good age to learn Latin. Just begin the journey. Your trip may take longer than others or you may finish in record time. Whether you reach the goal of mastering the Latin grammar in two years or four, doesn't really make much difference. The next part of the journey still awaits you, the excitement of reading real Latin and preparing to read the classics.

TEACHING GUIDELINES

Lesson Overview

These lessons are written for a class, but they can easily be adapted for one student. However, if you are a homeschooler I strongly encourage you to form a Latin class if at all possible. If you are learning Latin along with your child, then you and your child form a class, so be sure to include yourself in all of the recitations, games, quizzes, etc. If you can add a sibling or a cousin, you have a class of three! And you may want to consider recruiting a friend for your child to learn with, or even forming a cottage class for homeschoolers in your area.

A Full Week's Schedule consists of five parts:
A) Lesson
B) Workbook
C) Oral Drill
D) Quiz or Test
E) (Optional) *Lingua Angelica* and/or *Famous Men of Rome* or other Memoria Press history resources.

 A Lesson

Each lesson plan has four numbered sections.

❶ Opening, Recitation, Review
The short-term goal of each lesson is to put Latin into the temporary memory of the students. The long-term goal is to put Latin into the permanent memory of the students. This is achieved through recitation and review.

Opening, - The opening greeting should be done at the beginning of every class period.
1. Teacher: *Salvete, amici Latinae* (Hello, friends of Latin) or *Salvete, discipuli* (Hello, students) or *Salve, amice Latinae* (For one student)
2. Students: *Salve, magistra (magister)* (Hello, teacher - feminine or masculine form)

Recitation - A full recitation should be done at least once a week, more if needed. As the recitation grows throughout the year, you will want to divide it up into sections to recite over two or more days.
1. Teacher: *Súrgite* (Stand up) or (*Surge*) (For one student)
2. Teacher: *Recitemus* (Let us recite)
3. Recite Grammar forms: You may give the first word of the conjugation/declension as a cue word and let students complete the paradigm orally in a group recitation. You may lead the class orally in reciting the conjugations/declensions if you think students are shaky and need the reinforcement of hearing a strong and correct voice. You may ask individual students to complete a conjugation or declension.
4. Music and Prayers. If you are teaching music and prayers, they should be included in this recitation time. A music and prayer syllabus follows this section.
5. At the end of the recitation:
   Teacher: *Sedete* (Sit down) or (*Sede*) (For one student)

Review - A review time at the beginning of every class should include some or all of these components.
1. <u>Grammar Questions,</u> which are in both the teacher and student workbook appendix. The Recitation section of each lesson in the Teacher Manual lists the appropriate Grammar Questions to select from.
2. <u>Cumulative</u> vocabulary drill with flashcards. Pull cards randomly and going around the room, drill students from English to Latin and from Latin to English. Ask for conjugation, principal parts, declension, genitive singular, gender, etc.
3. <u>Cumulative vocabulary drill sheets,</u> which are in both the teacher and student workbook appendix. When you see vocabulary start to slip about the middle of the year, you will want to begin reviewing with these sheets. Instructions are on the first sheet. These sheets are an alternative to the flashcards.
4. <u>Form drills.</u> Immediate recognition of inflected forms is a major goal of the First Form Latin program. Use the forms in the Oral Drill in the text or draw a vocabulary card and make up your own inflected forms.
5. Latin Sayings. Draw flashcards and quiz around the room.

TEACHING GUIDELINES

Lesson Overview

2 Latin Saying
- Say the Latin Saying aloud and have students repeat after you. Discuss the significance of the Latin Saying as explained in the text.
- The learning objectives are for the students to be able to pronounce, write, and spell the Latin saying correctly from memory on the weekly quiz, and to remember all sayings at the end of the year.
- The vocabulary and grammar notes for the Latin saying are **FYI**, *for your information*. Use your judgment about how much of this information to share with your students.
- Learning Latin sayings is important. Review them often. Students enjoy them, and they become useful in explaining grammar and syntax as students advance in their Latin knowledge.

3 Vocabulary
- Vocabulary acquisition takes time and effort. Putting vocabulary into the permanent memory of students is more challenging than grammar forms. The failure to master vocabulary is the leading cause of student frustration with Latin or any foreign language.
- Pronounce words and definitions for students and have them repeat after you. For younger students you will want to write the Latin vocabulary on the board or overhead and have students write words in their notebooks. Older students can just work from the text.
- Vocabulary mastery is the learning objective. Students should be able to pronounce and spell each Latin word when given the English meaning and vice versa. Students should know the full dictionary form.
- English words that are derived from Latin words are called derivatives. Two different words derived from the same word are called cognates.
- Pronounce English derivatives and let students offer synonyms. If students can't come up with a good definition, then give them one. Use the derivative in a sentence.
- Let students offer additional derivatives if you have time.
- If a student offers a word as a derivative that you aren't sure of, look the word up in a dictionary.
- Learning to use the dictionary and look up the etymology of words is a valuable skill. Be sure to have a dictionary in your room that has word etymology.
- You have a limited amount of time for your Latin lesson. Learning derivatives should not take much time away from Latin. The purpose of the derivatives is to 1) help students remember the meanings of the Latin words and 2) build English vocabulary. Exposure, not mastery, is the goal for derivatives.

4 Grammar - Syntax
- Chalk Talk. The lessons are scripted for you, usually in the form of questions and answers. Use a board or overhead projector. Asking questions keeps the students attentive and interested. Approach the grammar lesson like a detective looking for clues. Ask students to compare, contrast, and analyze. (cca)
- FYI sections are grammar explanations for the teacher only. They are not meant to be taught to the students, unless you think your students are ready for some advanced work.
- Recite the grammar forms aloud several times as a class (*in choro*). Commit them to memory by the disappearing line technique.

Disappearing Line Technique
Write the conjugation on the board and recite *in choro* several times. Call on a few students to recite the conjugation individually.

amo	amamus
amas	amatis
amat	amant

TEACHING GUIDELINES

Lesson Overview
Disappearing Line Technique

Erase **amo** and recite the complete conjugation with students. Point to where **amo** was written and ask students what was there. Erase **amas** and again recite the complete conjugation with students from the beginning. Point to where **amo** and **amas** were and ask students what was there. Continue erasing one word at a time, reciting the complete conjugation each time with students, until the whole conjugation has been erased. Repeat again several times with students. Ask for a volunteer to stand and recite the conjugation from memory. Continue around the room until every student has recited. The purpose of the *disappearing line technique* is 1) to put the grammar forms into the temporary memory of the students and, 2) to show the students how quickly they can memorize if they concentrate. Only time and constant review will put the conjugations and declensions into the permanent memory. Their assignment after memorizing in class should be to go home and say the grammar forms ten times a day for the rest of the week.

Ⓑ Workbook

- The Workbook exercises have been carefully developed to ensure mastery. They are not just busy work. You and your students should approach each section of the Workbook as something to be done carefully, accurately, and neatly. You should check the answers before the student goes to the next section. Aim for about twenty minutes of quality written work per day.
- Do all of the Workbook pages. It's almost impossible to practice Latin too much. After students have written out some conjugations or declensions neatly in their workbooks, you *may* choose to do some work orally. If so, be sure your student is very accurate in his oral work and then let him/her put a check by that exercise and write *oral*. It is also acceptable to use ditto marks for meanings after the first lesson. Again, be accurate. Don't ditto words that aren't the same, like *walk* and *walking*, *am* and *is*.
- The Workbook exercises are generally organized into these sections:
     Word Study and Grammar
     Conjugations or Declensions
     Form Drills
     Translation Skills
     Enrichment~ Honors~ Review
- Each section logically follows the one that precedes it and prepares for the one that follows. The exception is *the last section*, which, except for the occasional "Honors" work, can be done at any time.
- The Workbook is not something to assign for homework or seatwork while you do something else. Do the Workbook together as a class.
- A good plan is to do half of a drill or exercise together until you are sure your students understand the concept. The rest can be completed as seatwork and checked immediately afterwards or assigned for homework and checked the next day.
- Require neat, legible handwriting in workbooks. Students who know cursive should use it. It is very important that students not be allowed to do sloppy, incorrect work, since that is inconsistent with success in Latin. Latin should develop accuracy, precision, and attention to detail.

Ⓒ Oral Drill

- The <u>Textbook Oral Drill</u> (most textbook lessons have one) should be used to assess grammar and vocabulary mastery. This is your final exercise at the end of the week, before the quiz.
- Do the Latin to English drill first. Skip around; do not do the numbers in order. Call on students randomly around the room to read a Latin word and give the English meaning. The goal is immediate recognition of the meaning of the inflected form.
- Do the English to Latin drill. This is much more difficult and students will be slower.
- You may want to use the Oral Drill as a timed written pre-test to assess student progress.
- The Oral Drills are on Disc 3 of the First Form DVDs.

TEACHING GUIDELINES
Lesson Overview

D Quiz

- There are several factors that determine how you administer and grade your tests and quizzes: age, ability, background, classroom instruction time. You must use good judgment in assessing the progress of your students. If you need to alter our quizzes for your situation, do so.
- Do not try to make your students fit a bell-shaped curve. It is always possible to give a test or quiz hard enough that only a few will do well, but that is not a way to assess student progress.
- If you have hardworking and conscientious students, you should give tests and quizzes that enable them to be successful. Quizzes and tests should be adjusted to fit your students and your situation.
- It is very important to remember priorities in teaching Latin. For beginners, the order of importance is listed below. If your student does well in the first two areas and less well in the last three, then you can still consider your class a success.
  recitation of model paradigms
  ability to decline or conjugate nouns or verbs in addition to paradigm models
  vocabulary mastery
  speed in recognition of inflected forms
  translation skills

E LINGUA ANGELICA SYLLABUS

If you can devote more than three hours per week to Latin, you should strongly consider memorizing prayers and music. Prayers and music develop vocabulary and pronunciation skills, and also provide enrichment and translation exercises in real Latin. Memorizing real Latin passages is a great aid in learning Latin and developing translation skills.

The following syllabus for including *Lingua Angelica* in your Latin program is very doable if you practice each memory piece several times each day and make memory work a priority. But if you need more time to learn each piece or if you find that you don't have time for this enrichment, that is fine. Learning Latin grammar is the first priority. It is better to do one program well than two poorly. If you decide to do *Lingua Angelica*, then you need to designate the time and complete the course. It is frustrating for students to start something and not have the time set aside to complete it. When your student has learned a selection, be sure to include it in each week's recitation time.

Unit I

Lesson 1	Dona Nobis Pacem
Lesson 2	Christus Vincit
Lesson 3	Table Blessing, Lines 1-2
Lesson 4	Table Blessing, Lines 3-4
Lesson 5	Table Blessing, Lines 5-6
Lesson 6	Review all

Unit II

Lesson 7	Signum Crucis
Lesson 8	Resonet in Laudibus, verse 1
Lesson 9	Resonet in Laudibus, verse 2
Lesson 10	Resonet in Laudibus, verse 3
Lesson 11	Resonet in Laudibus, refrain
Lesson 12	Resonet in Laudibus, Review all lines
Lesson 13	Review all

TEACHING GUIDELINES

Unit III

Lesson 14	Adeste Fideles, verse 1
Lesson 15	Adeste Fideles, verse 2
Lesson 16	Adeste Fideles, verse 3
Lesson 17	Adeste Fideles, refrain
Lesson 18	Gloria Patri, 3 lines, page 7
Lesson 19	Gloria Patri, 2 lines, pages 7, 8
Lesson 20	Review

Unit IV

Lesson 21	Pater Noster, page 12
Lesson 22	Pater Noster, page 13
Lesson 23	Pater Noster, page 14
Lesson 24	Pater Noster, page 15
Lesson 25	Pater Noster, Review
Lesson 26	Agnus Dei
Lesson 27	Kyrie (Greek)
Lesson 28	Review

Unit V

Lesson 29	Sanctus and Benedictus, 3 lines
Lesson 30	Sanctus and Benedictus, 2 lines
Lesson 31	Sanctus and Benedictus, 3 lines
Lesson 32	Review Units I, II
Lesson 33	Review Units III, IV
Lesson 34	Review all

Lingua Angelica Lesson Plan

If you are including *Lingua Angelica* you probably will want to sing/recite music and prayers during the greeting/recitation time. The workbook exercises can be done at the end of each day's work as outlined below or, if you prefer, all on Fridays. You may have time to do only part of the *Lingua Angelica* program. In order of importance the priorities are: (1) Memorization of the piece (2) Interlinear and English translation in workbook (3) Writing the lines 2X (4) Reciting vocabulary aloud (5) Vocabulary drill in workbook (6) Parsing

Day 1   Sing/Recite with CD and write assigned lines 2X.

Day 2   Sing/Recite with CD and recite vocabulary aloud 3X.

Day 3   Sing/Recite with CD and complete vocabulary drill. Parse words only if appropriate for your students.

Day 4   Sing/Recite with CD and do interlinear and English translation.

Day 5   Sing/Recite with CD. Quiz. There are six levels of testing that you can choose from on page xi of the *Lingua Angelica* teacher manual.

TEACHING GUIDELINES

Games and Review Activities

1) GLADIATORS – Divide the class into two opposing teams of 'gladiators.' Each team chooses a name (Roman, of course). One person from each team comes forward to compete. The teacher calls out a vocabulary word (in Latin or English) and the first student to write the word correctly spelled (with the genitive singular for nouns and the principal parts for verbs) gets a point for his/her team. At the end of the game, the team with the most points wins. This game also works well with the Oral Drills in each lesson of the text. Instead of a vocabulary word, give a form, and the first student to correctly translate it is the winner.

2) BOARD RACES – Several students are placed at the board (however many will fit) and they are given a word to decline or conjugate. The first person to complete the grammar form correctly wins and gets to stay at the board as other students come up to compete against him/her. This game also works well using the Oral Drill exercises in the text.

3) FLASHCARD FRENZY – Students are paired into teams of two. One student is handed a master set of vocabulary flashcards and a timer is set for 30 seconds. When the teacher says "go," the student with the cards calls out the first word in English. His teammate gives the Latin (including the genitive singular for nouns). The goal is for the team to get as many words as they can (correctly) in 30 seconds. If the person answering the questions doesn't know one immediately, the caller should move on to the next one. The purpose of this game is to stress mastery of the words with instant recall. The person in the class who gets the most words in 30 seconds is the winner. Always switch the teams off so that everyone gets an opportunity to compete. It is helpful to put a third person at the board to keep a tally of correct words.

4) LATIN PICTIONARY – I don't know if this game is a good use of time because you can't cover much material as quickly as you can with the other games, but the students do love it. Divide the students into teams of three or four per team. One person on the team will be given a vocabulary card with a word on it. He/she has to draw a picture depicting this word and his/her team has to guess the word (in Latin, of course). The other teams need to pay attention because if the first team doesn't get the word in 30 seconds, they will have an opportunity to steal the point. Have the other teams write down the answer they think is correct and give a point to each team that has the correct answer.

5) VOCABULARY/FORMS BEE – This game works just like a spelling bee. Line the students up in the front of the class. Give the first student in the line a vocabulary word or a form from the Oral Drill. The student has to give the Latin word orally. If the student cannot get the word, it passes to the next student. If that student gets it, the student who didn't get it has to sit down. If more than one student misses the word, they all have to sit down. The last student up at the end of the game is the winner.

6) LATIN JEOPARDY – This game requires some teacher preparation ahead of time. Have four or five categories of questions (vocabulary, forms, grammar questions, declining, conjugating, gender, etc.). Make an envelope for each category and place cards in it that say $100, $200, $300, $400, $500. On the back of each card, put a question having to do with that category. Obviously, the questions need to get harder as the value of the questions gets higher. Make a Jeopardy board on the chalkboard:

TEACHING GUIDELINES

VOCABULARY	FORMS DRILL	GRAMMAR	DECLINE	CONJUGATE
$100	$100	$100	$100	$100
$200	$200	$200	$200	$200
$300	$300	$300	$300	$300
$400	$400	$400	$400	$400
$500	$500	$500	$500	$500

Depending on the size of your class, this can be played individually or with teams. The first person or team gets to choose a category and a dollar amount. You pick the card out of the appropriate envelope, ask the question, and give 15-30 seconds for an answer. If the student or team answers correctly, they get the money. If they don't answer correctly, the money is subtracted from their total (they can go into a negative balance). If you want to do two rounds, you can double the money for the second round. Also, you can have a card mixed in somewhere that says "Daily Double," and whoever gets that question gets double the money. The person/team with the most money at the end is the winner.

7) LATIN MILLIONAIRE – This game is copied from "Who Wants to Be a Millionaire?" This game will take teacher preparation time. It can be played in teams or individually. Make cards worth $100, $200, $300, $500, $1,000, $2,000, $4,000, $8,000, $16,000, $32,000, $60,000, $125,000, $250,000, $500,000, and $1,000,000 with a question on the back of each card (getting correspondingly harder as the value of the cards gets higher). These should be multiple choice questions. For the sake of time, all the students can play together (either individually or in teams) and write their answers on paper or on individual white boards. You can keep score on the chalkboard. Every student/team that has the correct answer would get the money. At the end of the game, the student/team with the most money wins. You can use lifelines if you want to (more fun, but also more time-consuming) – ask the audience, 50/50, and phone a friend.

TEACHING GUIDELINES

Developing a Syllabus

Every teacher must develop a syllabus that fits his schedule and students. We recommend three hours per week and 33-35 weeks to complete First Form in one year for students in grades 4-6. Students in grades 7-up may complete First Form in less time, even in one semester. However, this schedule may not be realistic for your school or homeschool depending on many factors that affect learning success. The most important factors to consider as you develop your syllabus and lesson plans are:

1. Homeschooling or classroom. If classroom, how many students in your class?
2. Age, ability, and Latin background of students.
3. Time on task. How much time are you planning to devote to Latin each week and how many weeks are in your school year?
4. Experience and Latin background of teacher.

It is most important to remember that you should plan your course so that your students can be successful. Students who have normal ability and who are willing to work should make A's or B's. It is always possible to design a class so that only one or two exceptional students make A's and all other students fit the bell-shaped curve. This only drives students away and discourages capable students.

The goal of teaching is that you cover the material so well and review so often that everyone in the class has mastery of the material and should make A's on your quizzes and tests. There will always be the occasional student who will not work, but that is beyond your control.

Preparing to Teach the Lesson

Read the Teaching Guidelines on the previous pages. Now go back and read them again. Follow the preparation suggestions below and you will be successful.

Student Text and Teacher Manual
1. Each unit has an introductory page. Read over this page several times. It will familiarize you with important terms and concepts that will be covered in each unit. If you do not understand everything do not be concerned.

2. For each lesson, *read* and *reread* the student text and the scripted lesson plan in the teacher manual. There are additional grammar helps in the appendix if you need them. Listen to the audio and practice your pronunciation.

Workbook
3. Do all of the workbook pages for the lesson. Check the answer key and correct your errors.

Oral Drill and Quiz
4. Do the Oral Drill on the right-hand page of the text *after* you have completed the workbook. The Oral Drill is designed to be used as a final test to determine form mastery. Now take the quiz and correct your mistakes.

5. Now you are ready to teach the lesson. Do not be dismayed that you do not understand everything. Who does? As you teach the lesson and go over it the second time, your knowledge and understanding will grow.

What a great accomplishment to be learning and teaching Latin, a challenging subject that will improve your mind and the minds of your students.

TEACHING GUIDELINES

Sample Lesson Plan for Lesson VIII

Day 1	Recitation	5 minutes
	Teach Lesson Eight	
	Latin Saying	3 minutes
	Vocabulary	10 minutes
	Grammar	20 minutes
	Workbook Section I, V	15 minutes
Day 2	Workbook Sections II	30 minutes
Day 3	Workbook Sections III	30 minutes
Day 4	Workbook Section IV	10 minutes
	Oral Drill in Text	10 minutes
	Pre-quiz/test	20 minutes

If students show mastery in pre-test, the week's lesson is complete. If not, have students review and restudy material and give quiz again on Day 5.

TEACHING GUIDELINES

Pronunciation

There are many twists and turns to the pronunciation history of a very old language like Latin. The pronunciation of the ancient Romans, called the classical pronunciation, was modified by Christians in the Middle Ages, when Latin became the language of the church and of the educated class. You may see this pronunciation referred to by a number of names: ecclesiastical, medieval, Church, Christian, or Italian. This pronunciation is still used today in the Catholic Church, though very little since Vatican II, and in music schools for choral classical music, where it is slightly modified for the demands of open vowels in singing.

After the rise of modern languages, and the decline of Latin as a universal language, each nation's schools tended to speak Latin in their own native accents. In addition, after the Reformation, the British developed their own system which was slightly different from that spoken on the continent. To further confuse matters, 19th century scholars researched the pronunciation of the ancient Romans and introduced the *restored* (classical) pronunciation into English and American schools.

Ignoring all of these minor variations, however, the two main pronunciation systems for Latin are classical (restored) and Christian. They are very similar. Christian Latin is closer to modern languages, is used in classical music and Christian prayers, and sounds more beautiful to modern ears.

In my opinion, the confusion and damage of the forced introduction of the *restored classical pronunciation system* into English and American schools at the turn of the century was a significant factor in the decline of Latin in the school curriculum. Even today, the decision over which pronunciation to choose is an obstacle to the restoration of Latin in the curriculum of Christian and classical schools.

The differences between classical and Christian pronunciations are:

	Classical	Christian
Vowels:	long and short vowels long vowels are marked with a macron diphthong **ae** has sound of long **i**	long vowels only, not marked with a macron accent mark shows accented syllable diphthong **ae** has the sound /**ay**/
Consonants:	Latin **v** is pronounced like English **w** **c** and **g** are always hard	Latin **v** is pronounced like English **v** **c** and **g** are hard before **a, o, u** **c** and **g** are soft before **e, i, ae, oe** soft **c** has the sound of /**ch**/
	Consonantal **i** has the sound of the letter **j**	Consonantal **i** has been replaced by **j**

In practice, both in England and on the continent, the difference between long and short vowels has been ignored, all of them being given the quality of long vowels. The same is true to a lesser extent in America, where the difficulty of learning Latin in our lax culture makes the burden of trying to master very specific vowel sounds, for which English speakers do not have a good ear, an unrealistic goal. Most Latin teachers, in reality, have quite enough to do to teach Latin grammar and have, out of necessity, focused very little on the nuances of pronunciation. In reality, then, the only real differences between classical and Christian pronunciation that real students are likely to encounter are the letters **v, c** and **g**, and the diphthong **ae**. Not a big difference.

TEACHING GUIDELINES

Latin was and is a universal language. National languages do not have a standard pronunciation, a universal language even less so! English is now a universal language, and each nation speaks it with its own native accent. The desire to master a pronunciation of Latin that is foreign to one's native tongue is unnatural and a misplaced effort in the challenging task of learning Latin. There are many benefits to Latin study, but lowest on the list surely is the ability to speak it in some idealized pure form that few scholars have ever attained because someday you want to read the *Aeneid* exactly as the Romans did.

A fastidious concern about pronunciation is an impediment to learning a language. Those who will plunge in and speak a modern language learn much more quickly than those who are self-conscious about pronunciation. How much more so for a language that is learned through the grammar-translation method rather than the conversation method. The pronunciation guide in First Form is simplified for beginners so that pronunciation will not become an impediment to learning Latin grammar and vocabulary. As students progress in Latin, pronunciation tips will be added in a natural, incremental way.

The simplified pronunciation system for the First Form series is based on these principles:
1. The pronunciation system recommended is Christian but an audio with Classical pronunciation is available.
2. The difference between long and short vowels is not emphasized and long vowels are unmarked in the text.
3. For beginners, the most important question is which syllable to accent. In Latin there are only two choices, the penult (next to last) syllable, or the antepenult (second to last) syllable. In First Form, if the accent is on the penult it is unmarked; if the accent is on the antepenult it is marked with an accent mark.
4. Pronunciation tips will be added in successive books of the First Form Series.

First Form Latin

Student Text with Lesson Plans

CONTENTS

STUDENT BOOK TABLE OF CONTENTS

The Dauntless Three
from
Horatius at the Bridge

PRONUNCIATION

GREETING:

Teacher: *Salvete, amici Latinae*
(Hello, friends of Latin) or
(*Salve amice, Latinae*)
(Hello, friend of Latin)

Students: *Salve, magistra (magister)*
(Hello, teacher)

Latin pronunciation is very regular and easy so take heart, students, this aspect of Latin is probably easier to learn than in any other language.

WORKBOOK: Ask students to open their texts and workbooks and go through Questions 1-5 with them.

Long Vowels

The most important skill to teach here is the long vowel sounds.

In choro, recite the English vowel names in order:

(a)   (e)   (i)   (o)   (u)

and the Latin long vowel sounds in the same order.

/ah/   /ay/   /ee/   /oh/   /oo/

The only difficult thing here is that long **e** in Latin has the sound of English long **a** and long **i** in Latin has the sound of English long **e**.

Write on the board:

glória   **Jesu**
/gloh/ /ree/ /ah/   /yay/ /soo/

Pronunciation

Latin pronunciation is very phonetic and regular. There are two major pronunciation systems, Christian (ecclesiastical) and Classical. This text uses Christian pronunciation because it is closer to modern English, is used in classical music and Christian prayers, and sounds more beautiful to the modern ear. In practice, there are only a few differences between the two, the most notable being that *v* is pronounced *v* in Christian Latin, and *w* in Classical. So, *veni, vidi, vici* becomes *weni, widi, wiki* in Classical Latin.

Fortunately, written Latin is the same regardless of the pronunciation. The following guide is for Christian pronunciation, but a Classical pronunciation guide is in the appendix.

Alphabet

The Latin alphabet has the same letters as English except that it has no **w**. The letters **y**, **z** and **k** are infrequent and usually found in words of Greek origin. The Roman letter **i** was both a vowel and a consonant (similar to the English **y**). The letter **j** was added during the Middle Ages for consonantal **i**. Thus **Iulius** and **Iesus** came to be written **Julius** and **Jesus**.

Vowels

Latin has long and short vowels, but the distinction between them is not always observed by English speakers. In this text we will focus on learning the long vowels and the consonants only. You will notice on the audio some vowels that tend toward the short sounds, so the short vowel sounds are given below. In this text, long vowels will not be marked with a macron except for a few inflected endings. [1]

long	as in	sound	example	short	as in	sound	example
ā	*father*	/ah/	frāter	a	*again*	/uh/	mensa
ē	*late*	/ā/ or /ay/	sēdēs	e	*Ed*	/ĕ/	et
ī	*seen*	/ē/ or /ee/	amīcus	i	*it*	/ĭ/	cibus
ō	*open*	/ō/ or /oh/	nōmen	o	*on*	/ŏ/	novem
ū	*food*	/ōō/	lūna	u	*foot*	/ōō/	sum

A helpful tip to remember the five long vowels is to learn the two words, **glória** and **Jesu**.

The general rule for consecutive and double vowels is to give each vowel its proper sound with the following exceptions:

Digraphs		as in	sound	example
	ae and **oe**	late	/ā/	caelum, proélium
Diphthong				
	au	out	/ou/	laudo

6

(Many students have heard the Bach classic "Jesu, Joy of Man's Desiring.") When students learn the pronunciation of these two words they will have learned the five long vowels of Latin, plus the consonant **j**.

Short Vowels

The short vowel sounds are heard in some words such as **et** and **mensa**. The short vowel sounds of **e**, **i**, and **o** are the same as those in English. Students do not need to be concerned about these sounds, just aware that they will hear the short sounds occasionally.

Digraphs

A **digraph** is not a blend, but rather two letters that make one sound. Digraphs in English are **wh**, **th**, **sh**, **ch**, **ph**. Latin has only two major digraphs, **ae** and **oe**. Both are pronounced like the Latin long **e**, /**ay**/.

Diphthongs

A diphthong is two vowels that are blended together to make one continuous sound. The only diphthong to be learned is **au**, which has the /**ou**/ sound in *out*.

Consonants

The Latin consonants have the same sounds as in English except as noted below. The rules for hard and soft **c** and **g** are usually true in English and always true in Latin. Note that soft **c** and **sc** have different sounds in English and Latin.

c, g, and **sc** are hard before **a, o, u**, and **consonants**

hard c as in **c**at	/k/	culpa, clamo
hard g as in **g**o	/g/	fuga, gloria
hard sc as in **sc**out	/sk/	scutum

c, g, and **sc** are soft before **e, i, ae, oe**

soft c as in **ch**arity	/ch/	caelum
soft g as in **g**em	/j/	regina
soft sc as in **sh**out	/sh/	scio

gn as in canyon	/ny/	pugno
ch is hard as in chemistry	/k/	choro
j as in yes	/y/	Jesus
s as in **s**ing, never as in nose /z/	/s/	mensa
t when followed by **i** and another vowel	/tsee/	gratia

Accents

For the beginning Latin student, the most helpful information is not long and short vowels, but rather knowing what syllable to accent. In this text you will always know the accented syllable by following these easy rules. The last three syllables in a Latin word have names.

a mi cus

antepenult (2nd last)   penult (next last)   ultima (last)

Ultima comes from *ultimus*, meaning the last, or ultimate. **Penult** comes from *penultima*, meaning next to last. **Antepenult** comes from *antepenultima*, meaning before the penult.

Latin words are always accented on either the penult or the antepenult, never on the last syllable. In this text, if the accent is on the penult it will not have an accent mark, but if the accent is on the antepenult it will have an accent mark.

amicus   but   ámbulo

accent on the penult - no mark   *accent on the antepenult - accent mark*

7

WORKBOOK:
Complete Questions 6-8.

Consonants

The rules for soft and hard sounds of **c**, **g**, and **sc** are the same in English and Latin, the difference being that there are no exceptions in Latin and there are many in English.

Soft **c** and **sc** have the sound /**s**/ in English. (ceiling, scene) In Latin soft **c** is /ch/ and soft **sc** is /sh/ which are not sounds they have in English.

(In classical Latin **c**, **g**, and **sc** are always hard, never soft.)

The sound of **gn** is /**ny**/. Examples are *onion, poignant, canyon, lasagna*

WORKBOOK:
Complete Questions 9-16.

Accents (Students do **not** need to reproduce the accent marks in their written work.)
Knowing what syllable to accent is one of the most important helps to promote confident pronunciation. Vowels can range from long to short and no one will notice much but an accent on the wrong syllable is noticeable.

Write **a mi cus** on the board as it is above with the syllable names, and have students pronounce them with you. Recite them in the order **antepenult, penult**, and **ultima**. Think and say **APU** to help students remember the names of the syllables in order from left to right. (If you have trouble with these words you can use *last, next last* and *second last* instead, although these terms can be confusing.)

> Latin words are accented on either the antepenult or the penult, never on the ultima.
> In this text always accent a word on the penult, **unless there is an accent mark on the antepenul**t.

WORKBOOK: Complete Questions 17-24 with your students.

NOTE: Although Latin words are never accented on the last syllable, it is perfectly acceptable to stress the last syllable while learning and reciting conjugations and declensions. The goal of the beginner is to learn the inflected endings and how to spell them, so emphasizing and exaggerating those endings is natural and helpful. The correct accents marks are given throughout the text and you should observe them when teaching vocabulary and *try* to observe them in translation exercises.

UNIT I INTRODUCTION

① ORAL RECITATION/REVIEW

Teacher: *Salvete, amici Latinae*
      (Hello, friends of Latin)
Students: *Salve, magistra (magister)*
      (Hello, teacher)

Grammar Questions: 1-9
The Grammar Review Questions are at
the end of the workbook. Don't skip
this part of the review.

The Unit Introductions are designed to
give you and your students an overview
of the content of the unit. If you are
new to Latin, you are not expected to
understand the content of this page
completely.

② GRAMMAR - CHALK TALK

Students should have a Latin notebook
open for all lessons in case you have
anything you want them to write (notes,
practice exercises, etc.). Ask students
to read over the Unit I Introduction
silently before you ask questions.

Note to Teacher
Pay attention to your students. If
you ask them to write *conjugation*
in their notebooks two times, make
sure that they do it and that they

UNIT I INTRODUCTION

♦ In this unit you will learn *The Present System* of the *1st Conjugation* and the irregular verb **sum**.

♦ Latin verbs fall naturally into four groups or families called *conjugations*.

♦ Look at the conjugation of the present tense of the English verb *love*. Notice that the English verb *love* changes in the 3rd person singular which requires the ending **s**.

		SINGULAR	PLURAL
1st person	*(person speaking)*	I love	we love
2nd person	*(person spoken to)*	you love	you love
3rd person	*(person spoken about)*	he, she, it <u>loves</u>	they love

♦ To *conjugate* a Latin verb is to say or write its forms in an organized chart similar to the one above.

♦ The six attributes of a Latin verb are: *conjugation, person, number, tense, voice,* and *mood.*
In Latin, there are:

Four conjugations	1st, 2nd, 3rd, 4th
Three persons	first, second, and third persons
Two numbers	singular, plural
Six tenses	present, imperfect, future (Present System)
	perfect, pluperfect, future perfect (Perfect System)
Two voices	active and passive
Three moods	indicative, imperative, subjunctive

♦ In this unit you will learn about conjugation, person, number, and tense, but not voice and mood. (All verbs in this text are in the same voice and mood, *active indicative*.)

♦ Latin is a language of *stems* and *endings*. The three tenses of the Present System are all built on the *present stem*. The stem is the part of the word that doesn't change. The endings change for person, number, tense, voice, and mood.

8

spell *conjugation* correctly. Many students are careless and sloppy and will misspell words even when they
are copying from the board. Training in careful and conscientious work is an important part of education.
Students will raise their level of neatness and accuracy only to the level that you demand.

Scripted Lesson
Look at **Bullet 2**: Verb families in Latin are called? (conjugations) Write *conjugation* on the board and go over
spelling by breaking down into syllables (con ju ga tion). Ask students to write *conjugation* two times in their
notebooks. **Bullet 5**: What are the six characteristics (attributes) of a Latin verb? (conjugation, person, number,
tense, voice, and mood) How many conjugations are there? (four) Name them. (1st, 2nd, 3rd, 4th) How many
persons are there? (three) Name them. (1st, 2nd, 3rd) **Bullet 3**: Who is the 1st person? (person speaking) Who is
the 2nd person? (person spoken to) Who is the 3rd person? (person spoken about) **Bullet 5**: How many numbers
are there in grammar? (two) Name them. (singular and plural) Ask students to write *singular* and *plural* in
their notebooks and spell correctly. What does tense refer to? (time) What are the three dimensions of time?
(past, present, future) How many Latin tenses are there? (six) Name them. (present, imperfect, future, perfect,
pluperfect, future perfect) Recite tenses *in choro* (aloud together as a class) twice. What two attributes of verbs
will we not study this year? (voice and mood) What two words describing voice and mood will you see in your
book this year? (indicative active) You don't have to know what these words mean this year. You will learn
about voice and mood in Second Form.

WORKBOOK: Lesson 1, Complete Questions 1-6.

UNIT I
Verbs
1st Conjugation and Sum

Present System

Romulus, Remus, and the She-wolf
Capitoline Museums, Rome

This iconic statue of the ancient city of Rome depicts the twin brothers, Romulus and Remus, suckled by a she-wolf. The myth that the Romans were descended from ancestors so fierce and courageous they were raised by a she-wolf fits the national character of Rome, a city chosen by destiny to conquer and rule the world. Romulus founded Rome and became her first king, giving Rome its name.

9

Because all verbs in First Form are in the active voice and the indicative mood, there will be no lessons on voice and mood for students.

FYI (FOR YOUR INFORMATION)
VOICE: There are two voices in English and Latin, active and passive.
  Active voice: John <u>ate</u> the cookies.
  Passive voice: The cookies <u>were eaten</u> yesterday.
      In the active voice the subject performs the action of the verb.
      In the passive voice, the subject receives the action of the verb.
      In the passive voice, the actual doer of the action of the verb may be expressed by a prepositional phrase.
          Ex: The cookies were eaten <u>by John</u> yesterday.

MOOD: There are three moods in Latin. (Some grammars count the infinitive as a mood.)
      The indicative mood is used for statements and questions. Ex: I have Latin homework.
      The imperative mood is used for commands. Ex: Do your homework.
      The subjunctive mood is used for subordinate clauses, imaginary statements, exhortation, contrary to fact, purpose, etc. Ex: If I <u>were</u> you I <u>would</u> do my homework.   <u>Let</u> us do our homework.

     May, might, would, should, and *let* are helping verbs that indicate the subjunctive in English.
     The subjunctive is used very little in English, but is very common in Latin.

LESSON I

❶ ORAL RECITATION/REVIEW

Teacher: *Salvete, amici Latinae*
       (Hello, friends of Latin)
Students: *Salve, magistra (magister)*
       (Hello, teacher)

Grammar Questions: 1-16
(at the end of the workbook)

❷ LATIN SAYING

Say aloud and ask students to repeat after you.

in *preposition*	in	
chorus *noun*	together, chorus	
choro	*ablative sing. case*	
	2nd decl., Lesson 15	
récito *verb*	recite	
recitemus	let us recite	

FYI

Recitemus is the <u>subjunctive</u> form of **récito**. **Recitamus** means *we recite* and **recitemus** means *let us recite*. This use of the subjunctive mood is called an *exhortation*.

❹ GRAMMAR - CHALK TALK

On the board, recreate in three steps the First Conjugation chart of **amo**.

(Step 1) Write the English personal pronouns on the board leaving space as shown below for Steps 2 and 3.

In choro recitemus. *Let us recite together.*

First Conjugation - Present Tense
present stem   **ama-**

Person	Singular		Plural	
1st	am-**o**	I love	ama-**mus**	**we** love
2nd	ama-**s**	**you** (sing.) love	ama-**tis**	**you** (pl.) love
3rd	ama-**t**	**he, she, it** loves	ama-**nt**	**they** love

◆ **Amo** is our model to study *1st Conjugation* verbs.

◆ In the conjugation chart above the Latin *personal endings, o, s, t, mus, tis, nt,* are in bolded blue. The Latin personal endings correspond to the English personal pronouns.

◆ The *present tense* is formed by adding the personal endings to the *present stem,* **ama**.

◆ To find the *present stem* of each vocabulary word, drop the **o** and add **a**, the *stem vowel* of the first conjugation.[2]

Vocabulary

Latin	English	Derivatives
amo	I love, like	*amorous, amateur*
do	I give	*donate*
lavo	I wash	*lavatory*
nato	I swim	*natatorium*
oro	I speak, pray	*orator*
paro	I prepare	*preparation*
porto	I carry	*portable*
servo	I guard, keep	*conservation*
sto	I stand	*status*
voco	I call	*vocation, vocal*

10

Person	Singular	Plural
1st	I	we
2nd	you	you (pl.) or (all)
3rd	he, she, it	they

Teach the concept of **grammar persons**, as explained in **Bullet 5**. The **1st person** is the *person speaking*; **2nd person** is the *person spoken to*; **3rd person** is the *person spoken about*. Use example sentences: *I am the teacher; We are a class; You have done your homework; They are going home,* etc. A composition is always written in a particular person; most novels are written in the 3rd person, instructions are usually written in the 2nd person, an autobiography is written in the 1st person, etc.

(Step 2) On the board, write the conjugation of *amo*, as shown in the grammar chart, leaving a space between the stem and the blue **personal endings**. Point to each Latin personal ending and its corresponding English pronoun, so students understand that the Latin personal ending stands for the English pronoun. Ask students to identify the **root**, **stem vowel**, and **stem**, as explained in **Bullet 2**.

(Step 3) Complete the chart by adding the English meanings. Notice that the only time the English verb *love* changes is in the 3rd person singular.

Word Study • Grammar • Syntax

♦ There are three persons in grammar. Below are the English pronouns and the corresponding Latin personal endings. Notice that English has only one word for the singular and plural **you**.

		SINGULAR		PLURAL	
First Person (person speaking)		*I*	*o/m*	*we*	*mus*
Second Person (person spoken to)		*you* (sing.)	*s*	*you* (pl.)	*tis*
Third Person (person spoken about)		*he, she, it*	*t*	*they*	*nt*

♦ The Latin present tense corresponds to the English *simple present, progressive present,* and *emphatic present.* In English **amo** can mean:

I love	simple present
I am loving	progressive present
I do love	emphatic present

Oral Drill

they love	1.	**amant**	1.	he is swimming	natat
hsi carries	2.	**portat**	2.	they pray	orant
I guard, keep	3.	**servo**	3.	she washes	lavat
we swim	4.	**natamus**	4.	you are guarding	servas
you wash	5.	**lavas**	5.	he does give	dat
you (p) pray	6.	**oratis**	6.	we carry	portamus
hsi gives	7.	**dat**	7.	you (p) like	amatis
they stand	8.	**stant**	8.	we are calling	vocamus
we prepare	9.	**paramus**	9.	you stand	stas
you call	10.	**vocas**	10.	they prepare	parant

11

VOCABULARY
Say each word aloud with its meaning and ask students to repeat after you. Students should learn both meanings for a verb if two are given.
Pronunciation helps:
er in **servo** has the sound of *air*

Derivatives
See instructions on teaching derivatives in the Teaching Guidelines.

> *amateur*
> *donation*
> *stable*
> *station*
> *lave*
> *oratory*
> *transport*
> *export*
> *import*
> *conserve*
> *conservative*
> *vocal*
> *vocabulary*

GRAMMAR - CHALK TALK
**Memorize the present tense of
*amo***, its meanings, and the**
personal endings.**

Use the *Disappearing Line Technique* as described in the Teaching Guidelines.

Latin only has *one* form for the present tense. The English present tense has three forms:

> The simple present *I love*, which is a general statement not indicating specific time.
> The progressive present, *I am loving*, which indicates an action going on right now.
> The emphatic present, *I do love*, which is used for emphasis, questions, and negative sentences. English needs helping verbs to make negatives and questions.

You *do* love!	Do you love?	You do not love.

WORKBOOK NOTE: The workbook parsing and form building tables ask for the *entry form* which is the word given in the vocabulary list. (The *entry* word is the form listed in a dictionary.) **Hsi** is the abbreviation for **he, she, it** in the answer key. Students may use ditto marks in conjugations as shown in the workbook key. In all exercises and translations the English **you** is singular unless specifically identified as plural (p).

ORAL DRILL: After completing this lesson and <u>all</u> workbook pages, test the skills of your students by giving the Oral Drill in the text. See Teaching Guidelines for instructions.

LESSON II

① ORAL RECITATION/REVIEW

Teacher: *Salvete, amici Latinae*
      (Hello, friends of Latin)
Students: *Salve, magistra (magister)*
      (Hello, teacher)
Teacher: *Súrgite* (Stand up)
Teacher: *Recitemus* (Let us recite)
    personal endings (o, s, t, ...)
    amo - present tense
Teacher: *Sedete* (Sit down)

Grammar Questions: 1-19

② LATIN SAYING

Say aloud and ask students to repeat after you.

mater *noun*   mother *(Lesson 19)*
sto *verb*   I stand
  stabat   he/she/it was standing
(The personal pronoun *she* is not
expressed when there is a noun subject.)

- Unlike English, Latin does <u>not</u>
  have articles *the* and *a/an*.
- Latin word order is variable;
  the verb may be anywhere in a
  sentence. When we translate into
  English we use normal English
  word order: subject - verb.

The *Stabat Mater* is a very famous and
venerable Latin hymn. Students will
be impressed when they find it in a good college dictionary. The *Stabat Mater* is in the *Lingua Angelica* song
and translation books. The simple mournful melody and rhyming lyrics are easy to learn. Memorizing the *Stabat
Mater* is a good assignment or extra credit project, especially during Lent.

LESSON II

Stabat Mater   *The Mother was Standing*

First Conjugation - Imperfect Tense
present stem **ama-**

Singular		Plural	
ama-**bam**	I was loving	ama-**bamus**	we were loving
ama-**bas**	you were loving	ama-**batis**	you were loving
ama-**bat**	he, she, it was loving	ama-**bant**	they were loving

♦ The *imperfect tense sign* is **ba**. The *imperfect tense* is formed by adding the *imperfect tense endings*, **bam, bas, bat, bamus, batis, bant**, to the present stem, **ama**.

♦ *Imperfect* in Latin means *not finished*. The imperfect tense is used to describe an ongoing, repeated, habitual, or interrupted past action. It is never used to describe a single completed past action. Here are some examples of the imperfect tense in English.

I <u>was calling</u> you when the doorbell rang.   *interrupted*
I <u>used to call</u> home every week.   *repeated*

Vocabulary

Latin	English	Derivatives
aro	I plow	*arable*
clamo	I shout	*clamor*
erro	I err, wander	*erroneous*
juvo	I help	*adjutant*
laudo	I praise	*laudable*
narro	I tell	*narrator*
opto	I desire, wish	*option*
pugno	I fight	*pugnacious*
specto	I look at	*inspect*
tempto	I tempt	*temptation*

12

---

④ GRAMMAR - CHALK TALK

Ask students to analyze the conjugation chart in their texts and be prepared to help you explain it as you recreate
it on the board. (Give students a few minutes to look at their lesson.) Write *singular* and *plural* on the board. The
grammar persons will not always be written on a conjugation chart, so ask students what they are and where to
write them. Latin is a language of ? (stems and endings) What is the present stem? (**ama**) Write the present stem on
the chart in place for each person and number. What is the imperfect tense sign? (**ba**) Write it after each stem. What
are the personal endings? (**-o, -s, -t, -mus, -tis, -nt**) Write them in the chart. Which personal ending is different from
the ones learned in Lesson 1? (In the 1st person singular the personal ending may be **o** or **m**.) As you build your
conjugation chart, be sure to leave spaces between each component (**ama ba m**). Have students identify *stem (root
+ stem vowel)*, *tense sign*, and *personal endings*. Recite conjugation *in choro* in Latin and English.

Ask students to look at the English meanings and describe what kind of time they indicate. What does *imperfect*
mean in Latin? (not finished) What is the imperfect tense used for? (an ongoing repeated, habitual, or interrupted
action in the past) What is the imperfect tense never used for? (a one-time completed past action)

Word Study ◆ Grammar ◆ Syntax

♦ The Latin word **specto** means *look at.* Sometimes an English preposition is needed to translate a Latin verb.

♦ Because the personal ending of the verb is sufficient to indicate a pronoun subject, a Latin sentence may consist of one word. Read pages 93-95 for an English grammar review and instructions on sentence labeling and diagramming.

I was fighting.	**Pugnabam.**
You were shouting.	**Clamabas.**
We are washing.	**Lavamus.**
He plows.	**Arat.**

Stabat Mater is the name of an ancient Latin hymn, also called *The Dolorosa,* celebrating the emotions of Mary at the Cross. *The Dolorosa* has been set to many different lines of music, plainsong and melodic, and has been used in liturgy since at least the 14th century. Notice that the verb in *Stabat Mater* is in the imperfect tense, and precedes the subject.

Oral Drill

hsi was praising	1.	**laudabat**	1.	he was wandering	errabat
hsi praises	2.	**laudat**	2.	they plow	arant
they shout	3.	**clamant**	3.	she praises	laudat
they were shouting	4.	**clamabant**	4.	you were fighting	pugnabas
we help	5.	**juvamus**	5.	he was desiring	optabat
we were helping	6.	**juvabamus**	6.	we tell	narramus
hsi tells	7.	**narrat**	7.	you (p) look at	spectatis
hsi was telling	8.	**narrabat**	8.	we were helping	juvabamus
you look at	9.	**spectas**	9.	you err	erras
you were looking at	10.	**spectabas**	10.	they were praising	laudabant

13

VOCABULARY
Say each word aloud with its meaning and have students repeat after you. Students should learn both meanings for a verb if two are given.

Pronunciation helps:
1) **j** is pronounced like **y**
2) **gn** is pronounced like **ny,** as in *onion, lasagna,* or *canyon*
3) **ou** has sound of /ou/ in *out.*
Confusing words:
1) **oro** and **laudo** because they sound the same in English (prays and praise)
2) **aro**, **erro**, **oro**, and **amo** because they are short words with similar letters.
3) **porto**, **paro**, because students often confuse words that start with the same letter.
Derivatives:
Students who have read *Charlotte's Web* will remember the Arable family, who were farmers.

    adjutant, narration, narrate
    clamorous, exclamation, claim, opt
    errant, erratic, aberration, laud,
       tempt
    repugnant, spectacular, spectacle,
       spectator

GRAMMAR - CHALK TALK

What English helping verbs do we use for the Latin imperfect tense? (**was** and **were**) Ask students to give examples of English sentences where the Latin imperfect would be used.

Class Practice: Conjugate **laudo** and **pugno** in the present and imperfect tenses.

     Memorize the imperfect tense endings and the imperfect tense of *amo* with its meanings.

Use the *Disappearing Line Technique* as described in the Teaching Guidelines.

WORKBOOK: There are seven basic sentence types. Four are taught in this text. Go over pages 94-98 of the student text with students before you do Section V of the workbook.
FYI English and Latin tenses do not have the same names or corresponding meanings. The English meaning given in this lesson for the Latin imperfect tense is actually the English past progressive tense. It indicates an action going on in the past, but does not really convey the idea of a repeated action. A comparison of English and Latin tenses is provided in the text appendix on page 108, but it is not recommended for students to learn. Beginners should concentrate on mastering grammar forms and a standard English meaning. Advanced students will learn to translate ideas rather than memorized meanings.

LESSON III

① ORAL RECITATION/REVIEW
Teacher: *Salvete, amici Latinae*
      (Hello, friends of Latin)
Students: *Salve, magistra (magister)*
      (Hello, teacher)
Teacher: *Súrgite* (Stand up)
Teacher: *Recitemus* (Let us recite)
    personal endings
    imperfect tense endings
    amo - two tenses
Teacher: *Sedete* (Sit down)

Grammar Questions: 1-27

② LATIN SAYING

Say aloud and ask students to repeat after you.

in *preposition*	in	
umbra *noun*	shade, shadow	
ígitur *adverb*	therefore, then	
pugno *verb*	fight	
pugnábimus	we will fight	

Read the story of Leonidas in *Famous Men of Greece.*

In umbra, ígitur, pugnábimus.   *Then we will fight in the shade.*

First Conjugation - Future Tense
present stem **ama-**

Singular		Plural	
ama-**bo**	I will love	amá-**bimus**	we will love
ama-**bis**	you will love	amá-**bitis**	you will love
ama-**bit**	he, she, it will love	ama-**bunt**	they will love

◆ The *future tense sign* is **bi**. The *future tense* is formed by adding the *future tense endings*, **bo, bis, bit, bimus, bitis, bunt**, to the present stem, **ama**.

◆ The **i** in **bi** is inconsistent, being absent from the 1st person singular and changing to **u** in the 3rd person plural.

Vocabulary

adoro	I adore	*adoration*
ámbulo	I walk	*ambulance*
hábito	I live in, dwell	*habitat*
júdico	I judge, consider	*judicious*
laboro	I work	*laboratory*
líbero	I set free	*liberty*
návigo	I sail	*navigator*
óccupo	I seize	*occupy*
saluto	I greet	*salutation*
súpero	I overcome, surpass	*superior*

*Oral Drill for Lesson III is on page 110.

14

---

④ GRAMMAR - CHALK TALK

Write *singular* and *plural* on the board. Ask students for the grammar persons and where to write them. Latin is a language of? (stems and endings) Ask students for the present stem (**ama**) and write it in the chart six times. Ask students for the tense sign (**bi**) and write it after each stem. Ask students for the personal endings (**-o, -s, -t, -mus, -tis, -nt**) and write them in the chart. Ask students where the tense sign (**bi**) is altered. (missing in the 1st person singular, and changed to **u** in the 3rd person pl.) As you build your conjugation chart, be sure to leave spaces between each component. (**ama b o, ama bi s**) Identify the *stem (root + stem vowel), tense sign,* and *personal endings.* What English *helping verb* is used for the future tense? (*will*)

Class Practice: Conjugate **saluto** and **júdico** in the present, imperfect, and future tenses.

      Memorize the future tense endings, the future tense of *amo*, and its meanings.

Use the *Disappearing Line Technique* as described in the Teaching Guidelines.

Word Study ◆ Grammar ◆ Syntax

◆ To remember the tense signs for the imperfect and future tenses:

tense	tense sign	helping verb	vowel
future	**bi**	w<u>i</u>ll	i
imperfect	**ba**	w<u>a</u>s	a

In umbra, ígitur, pugnábimus. In August of 480 B.C., the Spartan king Leonidas with a Greek force of 7000 was holding the pass of Thermopylae against the much larger army of the invading Persian king, Xerxes I. The Greek historian Herodotus tells us of a Spartan soldier who, when told that the Persian arrows would blot out the sun, bravely replied, "So much the better, we will fight in the shade." The Latin translation is Cicero's (*Tusculan Disputations*, I,101). This phrase is the motto of the First Artillery Detachment of the United States Army.

Cicero
(Marcus Tullius Cicero) 106 BC to 43 BC
Cicero was a philosopher, politician, and Rome's greatest orator.

15

3

VOCABULARY
Say each word aloud with its meaning and have students repeat after you.
All verbs are 1st conjugation.

Pronunciation helps:
1) For words of three or more syllables, the accent is on the next to last syllable (penult) unless the antepenult is marked. Which words are accented on the penult? (**saluto, adoro, laboro**) On the antepenult? (**návigo, líbero, hábito, ámbulo, júdico, óccupo, súpero**)
2) *ambulo* and *saluto* - The vowel **u** is pronounced /**oo**/ as in *food*, not *you* as in *mule*.

Derivatives:
> navigation
> liberation, liberal
> adore
> habitation, inhabit
> ambulatory
> laborious
> judiciary, justice
> occupation

GRAMMAR - CHALK TALK
Students often confuse the imperfect and future tense endings. The tip in **Bullet 3** should help students keep them straight.

FYI
Conjugation is a Latin derivative meaning *join with*.
cum *with*
jugo, jugare *join*

Pay careful attention to the spelling of *conjugation*, which students often misspell.

NOTE
The syllable accented in the dictionary form of a word may change in its inflected forms. For example:
*ó*ccupo   The accent is on the antepenult.
occup*a*mus   The accent is on the penult, and thus it is not marked.

Just remember the rule and apply it to every inflected form.
Accent the penult unless the antepenult is marked.

LESSON IV

1 ORAL RECITATION/REVIEW

Teacher: *Salvete, amici Latinae*
(Hello, friends of Latin)
Students: *Salve, magistra (magister)*
(Hello, teacher)
Teacher: *Súrgite* (Stand up)
Teacher: *Recitemus* (Let us recite)
personal endings
imperfect tense endings
future tense endings
amo - three tenses
laudo - three tenses
Teacher: *Sedete* (Sit down)

Grammar Questions: 1-28

2 GRAMMAR - CHALK TALK

This lesson is for reviewing and
consolidating vocabulary and grammar,
as well as introducing the new concepts
of *principal parts* and the *infinitive*.
Ask students to number the bullets,
1-10, before you begin this lesson.

What are the three tenses in the Present
System and why are they grouped
together? (present, imperfect, future,
because they are all built on the
present stem) How many ways can
you write the verb **amo** in the **Present
System**? (18) Latin and English
dictionaries give an entry form for each

LESSON IV

First Conjugation - Present System

P.	S.	Present	Pl.	
1	am**o**	I love	ama**mus**	we love
2	ama**s**	you love	ama**tis**	you love
3	ama**t**	he, she, it loves	ama**nt**	they love
P.	**S.**	**Imperfect**	**Pl.**	
1	ama**bam**	I was loving	ama**bamus**	we were loving
2	ama**bas**	you were loving	ama**batis**	you were loving
3	ama**bat**	he, she, it was loving	ama**bant**	they were loving
P.	**S.**	**Future**	**Pl.**	
1	ama**bo**	I will love	amá**bimus**	we will love
2	ama**bis**	you will love	amá**bitis**	you will love
3	ama**bit**	he, she, it will love	ama**bunt**	they will love

Vocabulary Review

adoro adorare	*to adore*	**nato -are**	*to swim*
ámbulo ambulare	*to walk*	**návigo -are**	*to sail*
amo amare	*to love, like*	**óccupo -are**	*to seize*
aro arare	*to plow*	**opto -are**	*to desire, wish*
clamo clamare	*to shout*	**oro -are**	*to speak, pray*
do dare*	*to give*	**paro -are**	*to prepare*
erro -are	*to err, wander*	**porto -are**	*to carry*
hábito -are	*to live in, dwell*	**pugno -are**	*to fight*
júdico -are	*to judge, consider*	**saluto -are**	*to greet*
juvo -are*	*to help*	**servo -are**	*to guard, keep*
laboro -are	*to work*	**specto -are**	*to look at*
laudo -are	*to praise*	**sto -are***	*to stand*
lavo -are*	*to wash*	**súpero -are**	*to overcome, surpass*
líbero -are	*to set free*	**tempto -are**	*to tempt*
narro -are	*to tell*	**voco -are**	*to call*

* These verbs have irregular principal parts which will be explained in lesson 7.

16

verb along with its principal parts. What are principal parts? (Ask a student to read **Bullet 3**.) Look up the verb
walk in an English dictionary. What forms of *walk* are listed after the entry form? The dictionary should have
something like: *walk* (entry form), *walked, walking, walks*. (The fourth form *walks* is the 3rd person singular and
is not a principal part.) Start a chart of the principal parts of some typical English verbs. (Students do not need to
learn the names of the English principal parts.)

infinitive	present participle	past	past participle
(to) walk	(is) walking	walk**ed**	(have) walk**ed**
(to) work	(is) working	work**ed**	(have) work**ed**
(to) see	(is) seeing	saw	(have) seen
(to) drink	(is) drinking	drank	(have) drunk

Illustrate how we make all of our English tenses by using these **principal parts** and **helping verbs**. *I saw, I was
seeing, I will see, I have seen, I would have seen, I should have seen, I would like to see, I did see, I was seen, I
will be seen*, etc.

Walk and *work* are verbs with regular principal parts, and *see* and *drink* are verbs with irregular principal parts.
Ask for the principal parts of regular verbs *look* and *play* and irregular verbs: *give, do, come, ride, speak*.

Word Study ◆ Grammar ◆ Syntax

The Infinitive

- The present, imperfect, and future tenses make up the *Present System*. All three tenses are built on the *present stem*.

- In the Present System there are eighteen ways to write **amo**. A Latin dictionary does not list all of these forms, but instead gives four main forms for each verb. These four main forms are called *principal parts*.

- The *principal parts* of a verb provide the stems needed to conjugate that verb in all of its tenses. The first two principal parts of amo are

  amo   amare

- **Amo**, the 1st principal part, means *I love*, and is the first person singular of the present tense. It is the *entry form* of the verb in a vocabulary list or dictionary.

- **Amare**, the 2nd principal part, means *to love*, and has a special name, the *infinitive*. The *infinitive* of every 1st conjugation verb ends in **are**.

- The infinitive is used to identify the conjugation (family) a verb belongs to.

  > A verb whose *infinitive* ends in **are** belongs to the *1st conjugation*.

- The infinitive means **to** + the verb. The infinitive of **amo** is **amare** and means *to love*. From this point on, this text will use the infinitive meaning in the vocabulary lists.

- In a vocabulary list or dictionary entry a first conjugation verb may be written with its complete infinitive or with the infinitive ending.

  amo amare   amo -are

- The *official* way to find the **stem** of a first conjugation verb is to drop the **re** from the infinitive form. It is the infinitive that contains the **stem vowel, a**.

  amare   ama/re   stem = ama

- Say aloud the first and second principal parts of the verbs in the vocabulary review on the facing page.

17

What is the first principal part of **amo**? (**amo**) The second principal part? (**amare**)
What does **amare** mean? (*to love*)
What is the name of the second principal part? (infinitive)

(The names and principal parts for English and Latin verbs are not the same. The infinitive is the first principal part in English and the second principal part in Latin.)

What is the infinitive ending of a 1st conjugation verb? (-**are**)

How do you know a verb belongs to the 1st conjugation? (Its infinitive ends in **are**). Memorize this grammar rule.

Write **aro** and **erro** on the board and ask for the two ways a dictionary entry may be written.
aro arare   or   **aro -are**
erro errare   or   **erro -are**

Now that you have learned the infinitive, you see where the present stem is derived from. What is the *official* way to find the present stem of a 1st conjugation Latin verb? (Drop **re** from the infinitive)

Class Practice: Ask students to write the infinitive and meaning for **tempto**, **narro**, and **líbero**, and to show how to find the present stem of each. Calling on students around the room, say aloud the infinitives for all 30 verbs.

WORKBOOK NOTE: The last chart of the workbook for Lesson IV asks for a **synopsis** in the present system. A synopsis specifies a person and number and asks for verb forms in a particular set of tenses, voices, and moods. At this point the student only knows three tenses for the synopsis. Complete this chart in rows, not columns.

FYI
A **finite** (limited) verb is one that is specific in terms of person, number, tense, voice, mood. The **infinitive** (unlimited) verb form is not specific or limited to person, number, tense, voice, mood. The infinitive is the only principal part that has an easy-to-remember name.

(You may also see the infinitive listed as a fourth mood in some grammars.)

LESSON V

❶ ORAL RECITATION/REVIEW

Teacher: *Salvete, amici Latinae*
    (Hello, friends of Latin)
Students: *Salve, magistra (magister)*
    (Hello, teacher)
Teacher: *Súrgite* (Stand up)
Teacher: *Recitemus* (Let us recite)
    personal endings
    imperfect tense endings
    future tense endings
    amo - three tenses
    laudo - three tenses
Teacher: *Sedete* (Sit down)

Grammar Questions: 1-35

❷ LATIN SAYING

Say aloud and ask students to repeat after you.

civis	*noun*	citizen
Romanus	*adj.*	Roman
sum	*verb*	I am

Latin sentences have unpredictable word order, but the verb often comes last.

❸ GRAMMAR - CHALK TALK

What is the most common verb in English and Latin? (**sum**, the *to be* verb)
What kind of action does the *to be* verb show? (None. It shows *state of being* or *existence*.)

LESSON V

Civis Romanus sum.   *I am a Roman citizen.*

Irregular Verb **sum** - Present System
sum   esse

S.	Present	Pl.	
su**m**	I am	su**mus**	we are
e**s**	you are	es**tis**	you are
es**t**	he, she, it is	su**nt**	they are

S.	Imperfect	Pl.	
era**m**	I was	era**mus**	we were
era**s**	you were	era**tis**	you were
era**t**	he, she, it was	era**nt**	they were

S.	Future	Pl.	
er**o**	I will be	éri**mus**	we will be
eri**s**	you will be	éri**tis**	you will be
eri**t**	he, she, it will be	eru**nt**	they will be

♦ The *to be* verb, **sum**, is the most common verb in English, Latin, and many other languages. It is always irregular.

♦ The *to be* verb, **sum**, shows existence, not action. Notice that the personal endings are regular, although the infinitive, **esse**, and present stem are irregular.

♦ Forms of the *to be* verb, *am, is, are, was, were, be, being, been*, are helping verbs in English. Forms of **sum** are <u>not</u> helping verbs for the Latin tenses you have learned.

	Correct	*Incorrect*
I love, or I am loving	**Amo**	Sum amo
I was loving	**Amabam**	Eram amabam
I will love	**Amabo**	Ero amabo

*Oral Drill for Lesson V is on page 110.

18

Write the first two principal parts of **sum** on the board and pronounce for students. What is the name of the second principal part? (infinitive) What do you notice about the infinitive of **sum**? (It does not end in **are** like 1st conjugation verbs). **Sum** is an irregular verb. It does not belong to the 1st conjugation. Write the present tense of **sum** on the board or overhead and ask students to analyze. Are the personal endings regular? (Yes) What about the stem? (It changes) Repeat with the imperfect and future tenses. Are the personal endings regular? (Yes) What about the stem? (The stem changes again, this time to **er**.) **Sum** is an irregular verb because the stem is not constant.

Memorize the first two principal parts and the Present System of *sum* and the English meanings.

Use the *Disappearing Line Technique* as described in the Teacher Guidelines.

Write **amo** on the board and ask students for its three English meanings. *(I love, I am loving, I do love.)*
How do you say *I love*? (**amo**) How do you say *I am loving*? (**amo**) (not **sum amo**) Some students will want to use forms of **sum** as helping verbs as they are in English.
Write on board: English has helping _____. Latin has helping _____. (verbs, endings)
Teach the forms of the *to be* verb in English: *am, is, are, was, were, be, being, been.*

Word Study • Grammar • Syntax

♦ The *to be* verb is often a linking verb that links the subject to a noun or adjective in the predicate. When the *to be* verb is a linking verb it is similar to an equals sign.

Mary is a mother.
noun

Mary is beautiful.
adjective

Mary = mother.

Mary = beautiful.

> **Civis Romanus sum** is a formula that could be used by a Roman citizen charged with a crime by a magistrate who did not have the proper authority to try him. It was a direct appeal to the emperor. It was used by St. Paul to demand that the praetors of Philippi come in person to release him. The praetors, who had illegally ordered him flogged and thrown into prison, got nervous and tried to have him released in secret (Acts 16: 35-39).

Tunica
(Tunic)

Stola
(Dress)

Palla
(Cloak)

Toga

Calceus
(Men's Sandal)

Calceolus
(Women's Sandal)

Roman Family
Only Roman citizens could wear the Toga.

19

NOTE: You may want to begin spreading the content of the recitation over the course of a week or doing a recitation only once or twice a week.

GRAMMAR - FYI
Sum is an irregular verb because its present stem is not constant. Do not confuse an irregular verb and irregular principal parts. There are many regular verbs (**do, sto, juvo, lavo**) with irregular principal parts that belong to each of the four conjugations. There are about eight irregular verbs in Latin. **Sum** is the only one that will be learned this year.

GRAMMAR - FYI
English has many <u>helping verbs</u>.

We <u>should have walked</u> to the store.

Walked is the main verb and s*hould have* are the helping verbs. *Should have walked* is a <u>verb phrase</u>.

Here is a list of English helping verbs.
Forms of **be**: *am, is, are, was, were, be, being, been*
Forms of **have**: *have, has, had*
Forms of **do**: *do, does, did*
Forms of **may**: *may, might, must*
Other helping verbs: *can/could shall/should will/would*

Most English verb phrases are translated by <u>one</u> Latin word!

(The perfect passive system does have compound verbs of two words. Students will learn the perfect passive system in *Second Form*.)

LESSON VI

ORAL RECITATION/REVIEW

Teacher: *Salvete, amici Latinae*
    (Hello, friends of Latin)
Students: *Salve, magistra (magister)*
    (Hello, teacher)
Teacher: *Súrgite* (Stand up)
Teacher: *Recitemus* (Let us recite)
    personal endings
    imperfect tense endings
    future tense endings
    amo - three tenses
    voco - three tenses
    sum - three tenses
Teacher: *Sedete* (Sit down)

Grammar Questions: 1-37

LESSON VI
UNIT I REVIEW
First Conjugation - Present System
amo   amare

P.	S.	Present		Pl.	
1	am**o**	I love	ama**mus**	we love
2	ama**s**	you love	ama**tis**	you love
3	ama**t**	he, she, it loves	ama**nt**	they love
P.	S.	Imperfect		Pl.	
1	ama**bam**	I was loving	ama**bamus**	we were loving
2	ama**bas**	you were loving	ama**batis**	you were loving
3	ama**bat**	he, she, it was loving	ama**bant**	they were loving
P.	S.	Future		Pl.	
1	ama**bo**	I will love	amá**bimus**	we will love
2	ama**bis**	you will love	amá**bitis**	you will love
3	ama**bit**	he, she, it will love	ama**bunt**	they will love

Irregular Verb **sum** - Present System
sum   esse

S.	Present		Pl.	
su**m**	I am	su**mus**	we are
e**s**	you are	es**tis**	you are
es**t**	he, she, it is	su**nt**	they are
S.	Imperfect		Pl.	
era**m**	I was	era**mus**	we were
era**s**	you were	era**tis**	you were
era**t**	he, she, it was	era**nt**	they were
S.	Future		Pl.	
er**o**	I will be	éri**mus**	we will be
eri**s**	you will be	éri**tis**	you will be
eri**t**	he, she, it will be	eru**nt**	they will be

20

This lesson is for the purpose of review, consolidation, and mastery of vocabulary and conjugations.
Make copies of workbook pages to use as drill sheets and practice tests.

MASTERY GOALS FOR GRAMMAR AND VOCABULARY

1) Be able to recite and write the conjugation of the model verb **amo** in the present system with meanings.
2) Be able to recite and write the conjugation of any 1st conjugation verb in the present system with meanings.
3) Be able to recite and write the conjugation of **sum** in the present system with meanings.
4) Be able to translate and spell correctly all 30 verbs, Latin to English and English to Latin. Be able to write the infinitive of each Latin verb.
5) Give synopsis of any verb in any person and number in the present system.
6) Form drill mastery. Rapid translation of inflected forms from Latin to English and English to Latin.
7) Know Latin Sayings - Latin to English and English to Latin.

See Teacher Guidelines for Games and Review Activities.

There is a test for this unit.

1st Conjugation Verbs

adoro -are	to adore	nato -are	to swim
ámbulo -are	to walk	návigo -are	to sail
amo -are	to love, like	óccupo -are	to seize
aro -are	to plow	opto -are	to desire, wish
clamo -are	to shout	oro -are	to speak, pray
do -are*	to give	paro -are	to prepare
erro -are	to err, wander	porto -are	to carry
hábito -are	to live in, dwell	pugno -are	to fight
júdico -are	to judge	saluto -are	to greet
juvo -are*	to help	servo -are	to guard, keep
laboro -are	to work	specto -are	to look at
laudo -are	to praise	sto -are*	to stand
lavo -are*	to wash	súpero -are	to overcome, surpass
líbero -are	to set free	tempto -are	to tempt
narro -are	to tell	voco -are	to call

Irregular Verb

sum esse	to be

Latin Sayings

In choro recitémus.
Stabat Mater

Civis Romanus sum.
In umbra, ígitur, pugnábimus.

* These verbs have irregular principal parts which will be explained in lesson 7.

21

MILESTONE MARKER 1

Learning Latin is like climbing a mountain. It is important to look back at where you came from and celebrate what you have accomplished. At the beginning of your climb you knew nothing about Latin, and now you know 30 verbs and how to recite all of them in three tenses, the Present System. Learning the present system of the 1st conjugation is a milestone. You know what *conjugation, person, number,* and *tense* mean. You know the *present, imperfect,* and *future* tenses in Latin and English. You know the three forms of the English present tense. In the next section of our journey up the mountain you will learn the Perfect System of the 1st conjugation. Soon you will have another milestone marker to add to your map.

UNIT II INTRODUCTION

The purpose of the Unit Introductions is to give you and your students an overview of the content of the unit. You are not expected to understand all of the concepts, but it is helpful to have a quick introduction of terms and ideas that the students will be encountering.

The Unit Introduction also helps students to see the big picture, to see each lesson as part of a whole that all fits together. Learning is a journey. To look back at where you have been and look forward to where you are going motivates the student and gives encouragement for the work ahead.

UNIT II INTRODUCTION

♦ The six tenses of a Latin verb are divided into two systems: the Present System and the Perfect System.

♦ The Present System has three tenses: present, imperfect, and future.

♦ The Perfect System has three tenses: perfect, pluperfect, and future perfect.

♦ The Present System is built on the present stem. The Perfect System is built on the perfect stem.

♦ A dictionary entry for a Latin verb lists four main forms called the Principal Parts.

♦ The Principal Parts provide the stems needed to conjugate a verb in all of its tenses.

♦ A verb may have regular or irregular principal parts.

Model of the Forum

UNIT II

VERBS
1ST CONJUGATION AND SUM

PERFECT SYSTEM

The Forum Today

23

LESSON VII

1 ORAL RECITATION/REVIEW
Teacher: *Salvete, amici Latinae*
    (Hello, friends of Latin)
Students: *Salve, magistra (magister)*
    (Hello, teacher)
Teacher: *Súrgite* (Stand up)
Teacher: *Recitemus* (Let us recite)
    personal endings
    imperfect tense endings
    future tense endings
    amo - three tenses
    voco - three tenses
    sum - three tenses
Teacher: *Sedete* (Sit down)

Grammar Questions: 1-37

2 LATIN SAYING
Say aloud and ask students to repeat after you.

erro *verb*	to err
errare	to err
est *verb*	he/she/it is
	(see Lesson 5)
humanum *adj.*	human

3 GRAMMAR - CHALK TALK
Review the concept of **principal parts**.
Ask students for the principal parts of
these English verbs: *live, drink, ring.*
Ask students for the first two principal
parts of **amo, laudo, specto.**

LESSON VII

Errare est humanum.   *To err is human.*

Principal Parts, First Conjugation

♦ The *principal parts* are the four forms of each verb that provide the *stems* needed to conjugate that verb in all of its tenses. The principal parts of **amo** and their meanings are:

1st	2nd	3rd	4th
am **o**	am **are**	am **avi**	am **atus**[3]
I love	to love	I loved	loved

♦ To write the principal parts of regular 1st conjugation verbs, drop the **o** from the first principal part and add the regular endings **are, avi, atus**

voc **o**	voc **are**	voc **avi**	voc **atus**
clam **o**	clam **are**	clam **avi**	clam **atus**

♦ The 3rd principal part is the 1st person singular of the *perfect tense.* You will use it in the next lesson. The fourth principal part will not be used in this book.

♦ A dictionary entry for **amo** could look like this:

amo amare amavi amatus

But usually a dictionary or vocabulary will shorten the entry for a regular verb and write the entry one of two ways.
    amo -are   **or**   **amo (1)**

The **(1)** or the infinitive ending **are** indicate that the verb is 1st conjugation and that it has regular principal parts.

24

Write the endings for the regular principal parts of a 1st conjugation verb on the board and show students how to write the principal parts for **laudo** and **specto**, using the root and adding the endings.

1st p.p.	2nd p.p.	3rd p.p.	4th p.p.
o	**are**	**avi**	**atus**
laud o	laud are	laud avi	laud atus
spect o	spect are	spect avi	spect atus

Class Practice: Ask students to write the **principal parts** for **saluto** and **óccupo** on notebook paper. Say them aloud. Call on students around the room to say the principal parts of all thirty verbs in Lesson IV.
Irregular Principal Parts: There are a few 1st conjugation verbs that have *irregular principal parts.* These must be mastered thoroughly and the best method is to say them aloud many times. Write the first two principal parts of each of these four verbs (**do, sto, juvo, lavo**) on the board and point out to students that the first two principal parts are always regular so they need only concentrate on the last two. Write the 3rd and 4th principal part of each verb and analyze how they are different from the regular endings. Say them aloud several times and have students write them on notebook paper.
        **Memorize the principal parts of *amo,* the regular endings for 1st conj. principal parts,
        and the irregular principal parts of *do, sto, juvo,* and *lavo.***

24

Word Study • Grammar • Syntax

♦ Say aloud the principal parts for all of the verbs in Review Lesson VI.

♦ Some verbs have irregular principal parts. If so, the dictionary or vocabulary list will write out all of the parts. The best way to learn irregular principal parts is to say them aloud many times.

Learn these 1st conjugation verbs with irregular principal parts.

1st	2nd	3rd	4th
do	dare	dedi	datus
sto	stare	steti	status
juvo	juvare	juvi	jutus
lavo	lavare	lavi	lautus

♦ **Infinitive as subject.** The infinitive is a *verbal noun* and can be the subject of a verb as it is in this week's Latin Saying - **Errare est humanum.**

♦ **Complementary infinitive.** When an infinitive completes the action of a main verb, such as **amo, paro,** and **opto,** it is a *direct object* with a special name, the *complementary infinitive.* The infinitive may precede or follow its verb. This is *Sentence Pattern #2 on page 97.*

Amo ambulare.   I love <u>to walk</u>.
I love to walk

                      SP   V-t   CI

Laborare parat.   He prepares <u>to work</u>.
to work he prepares

> **Errare est humanum.** This proverb has no particular author. Variations of it were common in ancient literature as they are today. One variant says that "to err is human, but to persist in error is diabolical." Another says that "to err is human, and to forgive is divine."

25

GRAMMAR - CHALK TALK

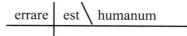

Bullet 7
Diagram the Latin Saying on the board to illustrate that **errare** is a noun subject of a sentence.

errare | est \ humanum

Hamlet's famous soliloquy has many infinitives. *To be or not to be, that is the question. Whether tis nobler in the mind to suffer the slings and arrows of outrageous fortune or to take arms against a sea of troubles and by opposing end them. To die, to sleep, to sleep, perchance to dream ...*

Bullet 8
What three verbs can be followed by an infinitive complement? (**amo, paro, opto**)
An infinitive that completes the action of a verb is a direct object. What is the name of this grammar construction? (complementary infinitive)

To show that word order is variable in Latin write these sentences with infinitives both ways.
        Amo ambulare.
        Ambulare amo.

Both sentences mean *I love to walk.*

FYI

The full and shortened names of the principal parts are provided for you, but it is not recommended that students be required to learn them at this time, other than the simple term, infinitive.

1st	2nd	3rd	4th
present active indicative (first person singular)	present active infinitive	perfect active indicative (first person singular)	perfect passive participle
present tense	**infinitive**	**perfect tense**	**perfect participle**

The 4th principal part can be written with the ending **-um** or **-us**. This text follows the convention of the *Henle* text and uses **-us**. The concept of principal parts is abstract and one that students have trouble fitting into their system of tenses and conjugations. Understanding will come as they see how principal parts are used.

Some sentences express a complete thought by means of a subject and verb only. *He sleeps. She thinks.* Most sentences, however, require one or more words in the predicate to complete the meaning of the subject and verb. These completing words are called **complements**. A complement can be a direct object, indirect object, predicate nominative, or predicate adjective. See Student Text, pp. 96-99.

LESSON VIII

① ORAL RECITATION/REVIEW

Teacher: *Salvete, amici Latinae*
Students: *Salve, magistra (magister)*
Teacher: *Súrgite*
Teacher: *Recitemus*

> **personal endings**
> **imperfect tense endings**
> **future tense endings**
> **1st conj. p.p. endings**
> **amo** - three tenses, p.p.
> **do, sto, juvo, lavo** - p.p.
> **sum** - three tenses

Teacher: *Sedete*

Grammar Questions: 1-41

② LATIN SAYING

Say aloud and ask students to repeat after you.
aut *conj.*   or

④ GRAMMAR - CHALK TALK

Perfect stem. What is the purpose of learning the principal parts of a verb? (So you can find the stems for all of the tenses) The three tenses you have learned were built on what stem? (the present stem) The next three tenses will be built on the perfect stem and are called the Perfect System.

nunc aut numquam   *now or never*

First Conjugation - Perfect Tense

perfect stem   **amav-**

Singular		Plural	
amav**i**	I have loved	amáv**imus**	we have loved
amav**isti**	you have loved	amav**istis**	you have loved
amav**it**	he, she, it has loved	amav**erunt**	they have loved

◆ The *perfect stem* is found by dropping the personal ending **i** from the third principal part.

amo   **amare**   **amavi**   **amatus**

amav/i   =   **amav**

◆ For the Latin verb, *perfect* means *completed*. The perfect tense describes a one-time action completed in the past.

Vocabulary

cras	tomorrow	*procrastinate*
heri	yesterday	
hódie	today	
non	not	
numquam	never	
nunc	now	
saepe	often	
semper	always	
tum	then, at that time	
umquam	ever	

26

As shown in **Bullet 1**, write the principal parts of **amo** on the board and show students how the perfect stem is found by dropping the **i** from the 3rd principal part. What is the present stem? (**ama**) What is the perfect stem? (**amav**) Compare the two stems. (The perfect stem adds the letter **v**.) (This is <u>only</u> true for 1st conjugation verbs with regular principal parts.) The present stem is used for what tenses? (present, imperfect, future) The perfect stem is used for what tenses? (perfect, pluperfect, future perfect)

Perfect Tense. Write the conjugation chart for the perfect tense on the board in two steps. Write the stem, **amav**, on the board six times and then add the perfect tense endings. Analyze the perfect tense endings. Write them on the board again as shown in **Bullet 3** and circle the personal endings (**-t, -mus, -tis, -nt**). In which two persons are the usual personal endings different? (1st and 2nd singular, **-i** and **-isti**) Pay special attention to the 2nd person singular and plural endings, -**isti** and -**istis**, which are easily confused.

Class Practice: Write the principal parts of **nato** and **servo** and find the perfect stems. Conjugate each in the perfect tense.

Meanings. Look at **Bullet 4**. What does *imperfect* mean in Latin? (unfinished or not completed) What does **perfect** mean in Latin? (finished or completed) What kind of an action does the imperfect tense describe? (a repeated or ongoing action in the past) What kind of action does the perfect tense describe? (a one-time action completed in the past)

Word Study • Grammar • Syntax

♦ The perfect tense is formed by adding the *perfect tense endings* to the perfect stem. The perfect tense endings are:

i	imus
isti	istis
it	erunt

♦ There are three English translations for the Latin perfect tense. For translation work any of the three are correct, although one may sound better in a particular context. For recitations use the *present perfect* meaning with the helping verbs *have* and *has*.

I loved	I have loved	I did love

> **Nunc aut numquam** is an old saying with no known origin. It is used as a motto by many organizations, such as the Netherlands Commandos.

Oral Drill

we have shouted	1. **clamávimus**	1.	we have judged	judicávimus
I have loved	2. **amavi**	2.	they have sailed	navigaverunt
you (p) have guarded	3. **servavistis**	3.	I have worked	laboravi
they have overcome	4. **superaverunt**	4.	she has given	dedit
hsi has walked	5. **ambulavit**	5.	you (p) have prepared	paravistis
you have prayed	6. **oravisti**	6.	he has washed	lavit
they have given	7. **dederunt**	7.	it has helped	juvit
I have erred	8. **erravi**	8.	I have told	narravi
you (p) have stood	9. **stetistis**	9.	they have shouted	clamaverunt
hsi has praised	10. **laudavit**	10.	we have fought	pugnávimus

27

VOCABULARY

Say each word aloud with its meaning and have students repeat after you.

Latin words without English cognates are more difficult for students to learn. Students are good at coming up with fun ways to connect a Latin word to its meaning, however. Teach **heri**, **hódie**, and **cras** as a unit and the rest of the words as pairs (*now, then; never, ever; always, often*).

Pronunciation helps:
The vowel team **ae** in **saepe** has the sound of /**ey**/ in *they*.

GRAMMAR - CHALK TALK

The primary meanings for the perfect tense are given in the grammar chart.

Look at **Bullet 3**.
Write *I have loved* on the board, and ask a student to complete the conjugation as you write it on the board. (you have loved, he <u>has</u> loved, we have loved, you have loved, they have loved) In what form does the helping verb change? (3rd person singular - *has* instead of *have*)

Memorize the perfect tense endings, the perfect tense of *amo*, and the three English meanings.

GRAMMAR - FYI

I loved is the *simple past*, **I did love** is the *emphatic past*, **I have loved** is the *present perfect*. The *present perfect* tense in English describes either an action of no definite time in the past or one completed in the present. As explained before, there isn't a one-to-one correspondence between the names and meanings of tenses in different languages. For instance:

> Caesar walked to the Forum on the ides of March.
> Caesar walked to the Forum every day.

The first sentence describes a one time completed action and would be translated by the perfect tense in Latin. The second sentence describes a repeated action and would be translated by the imperfect tense in Latin. In English, however, the past tense is used for both actions. You can consult the appendix for a comparison between English and Latin tenses, but teaching this to students is not recommended. At this point it is important that students simply memorize meanings for each tense that they learn. A thorough understanding will not be needed until translation of real Latin literature is begun.

LESSON IX

1 ORAL RECITATION/REVIEW
Teacher: *Salvete, amici Latinae*
Students: *Salve, magistra (magister)*
Teacher: *Súrgite*
Teacher: *Recitemus*

> **personal endings**
> **imperfect tense endings**
> **future tense endings**
> **perfect tense endings**
> **1st conj. p.p. endings**
> **amo** - four tenses, p.p.
> **do, sto, juvo, lavo** - p.p.
> **sum** - three tenses

Teacher: *Sedete*

Grammar Questions: 1-47

2 LATIN SAYING
Say aloud and students repeat after you.

semper *adv.*   always
fidelis *adj.*   faithful

Since this has become a well-known motto in English, it has been Anglicized in its pronunciation. It is often seen as Semper Fi. (/sem/ /per/ /fy/)

LESSON IX

semper fidelis   *always faithful*

First Conjugation - Pluperfect Tense

perfect stem   **amav-**

Singular		Plural	
amáv **eram**	I had loved	amav **eramus**	we had loved
amáv **eras**	you had loved	amav **eratis**	you had loved
amáv **erat**	he, she, it had loved	amáv **erant**	they had loved

♦ The pluperfect tense is formed by adding the *pluperfect tense endings* to the perfect stem. The pluperfect tense endings are identical to the imperfect of **sum**.

> eram   eramus
> eras   eratis
> erat   erant

Vocabulary

accuso (1)	to accuse	*accusation*
celo (1)	to hide	*conceal*
dúbito (1)	to doubt	*dubious*
muto (1)	to change	*mutate*
nego (1)	to deny	*negative*
perturbo (1)	to disturb	*perturb*
puto (1)	to think	*computer*
rogo (1)	to ask	*interrogative*
spero (1)	to hope	*despair*
volo (1)	to fly	*volley, volatile*

*Oral Drill for Lesson IX is on page 111.

28

---

4 GRAMMAR - CHALK TALK
Pluperfect Tense. What is the perfect stem of **amo**? (**amav**) How do you find the perfect stem? (Drop **i** from the 3rd principal part.) Write **amav** on the board six times. Analyze the pluperfect tense endings. (They are the same as the imperfect tense of **sum**) Write the *pluperfect tense endings* on the board. Recite conjugation *in choro*.

Meanings. Compare the helping verbs for the perfect and pluperfect tenses. (**have/has** for the perfect and **had** for the pluperfect) Look at **Bullet 2**. What kind of action does the pluperfect tense describe? (The pluperfect tense describes a past action completed prior to another past action.)

> A soothsayer had warned Caesar before he entered the Forum.

Class Practice: Write the principal parts of **puto** and **rogo** and find the perfect stems. Conjugate each in the pluperfect tense.

> ****Memorize the pluperfect tense endings, the pluperfect tense of *amo*, and the meanings.****

Word Study ♦ Grammar ♦ Syntax

♦ The pluperfect tense describes a past action completed prior to another past action.

Caesar *had conquered* the Gauls before he crossed the Rubicon.

I *had finished* my homework when the doorbell rang.

♦ The pluperfect tense is translated into English by the helping verb **had**.

Semper fidelis is the well-known motto of the United States Marine Corps. Marines often use the short form "Semper Fi" as a salutation to one another.

Galea
(Helmet)

Scutum
(Shield)

Pilum
(Spear)

Gladius
(Short Sword)

Caligulae
(Sandals)

Roman Legionary

29

VOCABULARY ③

Say each word aloud with its meaning and have students repeat after you.

Pronunciation helps:

Celo - The letter **c** is soft before **e, i, ae,** and **oe**, and has the sound of /**ch**/.

Rogo, nego - The letter **g** is hard before **a, o, u** and consonants, and soft before **e, i, ae,** and **oe.**

Puto, dúbito, muto, accuso -
poo toh   not   pyou toh

Remember the number (**1**) after the verb means that it is a 1st conjugation verb with regular principal parts.

From this point on verbs will be given with the infinitive meaning rather than the 1st person singular meaning. *To think* rather than *I think.*

Derivatives:
   compute, computation, reputation
   mutant
   interrogate
   volatile
   desperate
   indubitable
   negate
   accuse

NOTE: This is a good time to begin the vocabulary drill sheets in the back of the student workbook. Instructions for using these sheets are located there also.

ORAL DRILL: Lessons 3, 5, 9, 10, 14, 18, 22, 32 do not have Oral Drills. Oral drills are important as final assessments before quizzes and tests. For the lessons without oral drills, make up your own drills based on the examples in the lessons that have them.

LESSON X

❶ ORAL RECITATION/REVIEW

Teacher: *Salvete, amici Latinae*
Students: *Salve, magistra (magister)*
Teacher: *Súrgite*
Teacher: *Recitemus*

    personal endings
    tense endings - 4 tenses
    1st conj. p.p. endings
    amo - five tenses, p.p.
    do, sto, juvo, lavo - p.p.
    sum - three tenses

Teacher: *Sedete*

Grammar Questions: 1-51

❷ LATIN SAYING

Say aloud and ask students to repeat after you.

fortuna *noun*	fortune, luck
juvo *verb*	help, aid
fortis *adj.*	brave
fortes *(pl.)*	

Adjectives can be used as nouns to indicate a class of people, *the brave* or *the poor*. Remember, Latin does not have articles to signal that an adjective is being used as a noun. Notice the word order:

    direct object - subject - verb

Fortes fortuna juvat.   *Fortune aids the brave.*

First Conjugation - Future Perfect Tense

perfect stem   **amav-**

Singular		Plural	
amáv **ero**	I will have loved	amav **érimus**	we will have loved
amáv **eris**	you will have loved	amav **éritis**	you will have loved
amáv **erit**	hsi will have loved	amáv **erint**	they will have loved

◆ The *future perfect tense* is formed by adding the *future perfect tense endings* to the perfect stem. The future perfect tense endings are the same as the future of **sum**, excepting the 3rd person plural.

ero	erimus
eris	eritis
erit	<u>erint</u>

Vocabulary

appello (1)	to address	*appeal*
creo (1)	to create	*create*
culpo (1)	to blame	*culprit, culpable*
delecto (1)	to delight, please	*delectable*
demonstro (1)	to show, point out	*demonstrate*
exploro (1)	to explore	*explore*
exspecto (1)	to wait for, expect	*expect*
núntio (1)	to report	*announce*
oppugno (1)	to attack	*pugnacious*
vúlnero (1)	to wound	*vulnerable*

Oral Drill for Lesson X is on page 111.

30

---

❹ GRAMMAR - CHALK TALK

Future Perfect Tense. What is the perfect stem of **amo**? (**amav**) How do you find the perfect stem? (Drop **i** from the 3rd principal part.) Write **amav** on the board six times. Analyze the future perfect tense endings. (They are the same as the future tense of **sum**, *except* in the 3rd person plural) Write the *future perfect tense endings* on the board. Recite conjugation and meanings *in choro*.

Meanings. What English helping verbs are needed to translate the Latin future perfect? (*will have* or *shall have*) Look at **Bullet 2**. What kind of action does the future perfect tense describe? (The future perfect tense describes a future action completed prior to another future action.)

Class Practice: Write the principal parts of **demonstro** and **culpo** and find the perfect stems. Conjugate each in the future perfect tense.

    Memorize the future perfect tense endings, the future perfect tense of *amo*, and the meanings.

Word Study • Grammar • Syntax

♦ The future perfect tense describes a future action that will be completed prior to another future action.

By the end of this course <u>you will have learned</u> two conjugations and all five declensions.

Fortes fortuna juvat. This phrase was coined by the Roman playwright Terence and adapted by Vergil in the *Aeneid*, Book X, line 284. It is currently used as the motto of the 3rd Regiment of the U.S. Marine Corps.

Vergil
(Publius Vergilius Maro) 70 -19 BC
The author of Rome's great epic poem, the *Aeneid*

31

VOCABULARY
Say each word aloud with its meaning and have students repeat after you.

Notice the spelling of *exspecto* includes the letter **s**: ex + specto. Help students to spell each correctly.

English   expect
Latin   exspecto

Pronunciation helps:
gn as in *lasagna*
t when followed by **i** and a vowel
is /**tsee**/

Derivatives:
      demonstrative
      pronounce, Annunciation
      invulnerable
      exploratory
      culpable
      recreation
      expect, expectation
      delight

Note: wh = *will have*

GRAMMAR - CHALK TALK
The Perfect System is now complete. Name the three tenses built on the perfect stem. (perfect, pluperfect, future perfect) What does *perfect* mean in Latin? (completed)

Students will confuse the 3rd person pl. of the perfect system tenses. The perfect ending -**erunt** seems like it should be the future perfect ending -**erint**, and vice versa.

perfect	amav<u>erunt</u>	they loved
pluperfect	amáv<u>erant</u>	they had loved
future perfect	amáv<u>erint</u>	they will have loved

LESSON XI

1 **ORAL RECITATION/REVIEW**

Teacher: *Salvete, amici Latinae*
Students: *Salve, magistra (magister)*
Teacher: *Súrgite* (Stand up)
Teacher: *Recitemus (Let us recite)*
    personal endings
    tense endings - 5 tenses
    amo - six tenses, p.p.
    do, sto, juvo, lavo - p.p.
    sum - three tenses
Teacher: *Sedete*

Grammar Questions: 1-56

2 **LATIN SAYING**

Say aloud and students repeat after you.

et *conj.*   and

Ora and **labora** are the *imperative* forms of **oro** and **laboro**. An imperative form is used for a *command*. The imperative mood is not covered in this book.

Ora et labora.   *Pray and work.*

Irregular Verb **sum**
Perfect System

perfect stem   **fu-**

S.	Perfect		Pl.	
fu **i**	I have been		fú **imus**	we have been
fu **isti**	you have been		fu **istis**	you have been
fu **it**	he, she, it has been		fu **erunt**	they have been
S.	Pluperfect		Pl.	
fú **eram**	I had been		fu **eramus**	we had been
fú **eras**	you had been		fu **eratis**	you had been
fú **erat**	he, she, it had been		fú **erant**	they had been
S.	Future Perfect		Pl.	
fú **ero**	I will have been		fu **érimus**	we will have been
fú **eris**	you will have been		fu **éritis**	you will have been
fú **erit**	he, she, it will have been		fú **erint**	they will have been

♦ The principal parts of **sum** are irregular. The perfect stem of **sum** is **fu**.

    sum   **esse**   **fui**   **futurus**
              fu / i

♦ The perfect system endings of **sum** are regular.

32

---

3 **GRAMMAR - CHALK TALK**

Perfect Stem and Perfect System of Sum

What are the principal parts of **sum**? (**sum, esse, fui, futurus**) What conjugation is **sum**? (**Sum** is irregular and is not assigned to any of the four conjugations.) What is **sum** called in English? (the *to be* verb) What kind of action does **sum** show? (**Sum** does not show action; it shows existence or state of being.) What is the present stem of **sum**? (There is no present stem of **sum** because it changes, which is why **sum** is an irregular verb.)

Look at the Perfect System of **sum** and decide whether **sum** has a perfect stem. (Yes) What is the perfect stem of **sum** and how do you find it? (The perfect stem of **sum** is **fu**, which is found by removing the **i** from the 3rd principal part) Is the perfect stem of **sum** regular? (Yes, the stem is constant and the endings are regular.)

Recite *in choro* the present and the perfect systems of **sum**.

Meanings. Look at the meanings of the perfect system of **sum**. Compare the helping verbs to **amo**. (The helping verbs are the same.)

Word Study ◆ Grammar ◆ Syntax

Ora et labora. St. Benedict has been called one of the founders of Western Civilization, and even the *Father of Europe*. In 530 A.D., while the barbarians were fighting over Rome, St. Benedict and a small band of monks established a monastery at Monte Cassino, eighty-five miles southeast of Rome. The monasteries were oases of peace and learning during these dark ages, the cells that preserved the Christian faith and civilization until the ravages of the barbarians ended. St. Benedict's famous Rule for the life of monks became the basis for all monastic life which spread across Europe in the following centuries. *Ora et labora* is a summary of the Rule of St. Benedict and is a good rule for our lives, too.

Oral Drill

we have been	1.	**fúimus**	1.	I have been	fui
we had been	2.	**fueramus**	2.	you had been	fúeras
we will have (wh) been	3.	**fuérimus**	3.	we have been	fúimus
I have been	4.	**fui**	4.	she has been	fuit
I had been	5.	**fúeram**	5.	they have been	fuerunt
they have been	6.	**fuerunt**	6.	you (p) will have been	fuéritis
they wh been	7.	**fúerint**	7.	he will have been	fúerit
hsi had been	8.	**fúerat**	8.	we had been	fueramus
hsi wh been	9.	**fúerit**	9.	I had been	fúeram
you have been	10.	**fuisti**	10.	they will have been	fúerint

33

Memorize the perfect system of *sum* and the meanings.

GRAMMAR - FYI
The problem with learning meanings for Latin tenses is the lack of correspondence with the English tense system at certain points. The perfect of **sum** can also be translated *I was, you were, he was*, etc., depending on the context.

LESSON XII

ORAL RECITATION/REVIEW
Teacher: *Salvete, amici Latinae*
Students: *Salve, magistra (magister)*
Teacher: *Súrgite*
Teacher: *Recitemus*

    personal endings
    tense endings - 5 tenses
    amo - six tenses, p.p.
    do, sto, juvo, lavo - p.p.
    sum - six tenses, p.p.

Teacher: *Sedete*

Grammar Questions: 1-56

LESSON XII

UNIT II REVIEW

Perfect System 1st Conjugation - amo

perfect stem   **amav-**

S.	Perfect	Pl.	
amav**i**	I have loved	amáv**imus**	we have loved
amav**isti**	you have loved	amav**istis**	you have loved
amav**it**	he, she, it has loved	amav**erunt**	they have loved
S.	**Pluperfect**	**Pl.**	
amáv**eram**	I had loved	amav**eramus**	we had loved
amáv**eras**	you had loved	amav**eratis**	you had loved
amáv**erat**	he, she, it had loved	amáv**erant**	they had loved
S.	**Future Perfect**	**Pl.**	
amáv**ero**	I will have loved	amav**érimus**	we will have loved
amáv**eris**	you will have loved	amáv**éritis**	you will have loved
amáv**erit**	he, she, it will have loved	amáv**erint**	they will have loved

Perfect System - Irregular Verb sum

perfect stem   **fu-**

S.	Perfect	Pl.	
fu**i**	I have been	fú**imus**	we have been
fu**isti**	you have been	fu**istis**	you have been
fu**it**	he, she, it has been	fu**erunt**	they have been
S.	**Pluperfect**	**Pl.**	
fú**eram**	I had been	fu**eramus**	we had been
fú**eras**	you had been	fu**eratis**	you had been
fú**erat**	he, she, it had been	fú**erant**	they had been
S.	**Future Perfect**	**Pl.**	
fú**ero**	I will have been	fu**érimus**	we will have been
fú**eris**	you will have been	fu**éritis**	you will have been
fú**erit**	he, she, it will have been	fú**erint**	they will have been

34

This lesson is for the purpose of review, consolidation, and mastery of vocabulary and conjugations. Make copies of workbook pages to use as drill sheets and practice tests.

MASTERY GOALS FOR GRAMMAR AND VOCABULARY
1) Be able to recite and write the conjugation of the model verb **amo** in the Perfect System with meanings.
2) Be able to recite and write the conjugation of any 1st conjugation verb in the Perfect System with meanings.
3) Be able to recite and write the conjugation of **sum** in the Perfect System with meanings.
4) Be able to translate and spell correctly 20 new verbs and 10 adverbs, Latin to English and English to Latin.
5) Be able to recite and write the principal parts of each regular Latin verb.
6) Be able to recite and write the irregular principal parts of **do, sto, lavo, juvo** and the irregular verb **sum**.
7) Be able to give a synopsis of any verb in any person and number in the perfect system.
8) Form drill mastery. Rapid translation of inflected forms from Latin to English and English to Latin.
9) Know Latin Sayings - Latin to English and English to Latin.

See Teacher Guidelines for Games and Review Activities.

There is a test for this unit.

Verbs

accuso (1)	*to accuse*	**muto (1)**	*to change*
appello (1)	*to address*	**nego (1)**	*to deny*
celo (1)	*to hide*	**núntio (1)**	*to report*
creo (1)	*to create*	**oppugno (1)**	*to attack*
culpo (1)	*to blame*	**perturbo (1)**	*to disturb*
delecto (1)	*to delight, please*	**puto (1)**	*to think*
demonstro (1)	*to show, point out*	**rogo (1)**	*to ask*
dúbito (1)	*to doubt*	**spero (1)**	*to hope*
exploro (1)	*to explore*	**volo (1)**	*to fly*
exspecto (1)	*to wait for, expect*	**vúlnero (1)**	*to wound*

Principal Parts

1st	2nd	3rd	4th
am o	am are	am avi	am atus
I love	*to love*	*I loved*	*loved*
do	dare	dedi	datus
sto	stare	steti	status
juvo	juvare	juvi	jutus
lavo	lavare	lavi	lautus
sum	esse	fui	futurus

Adverbs

cras	*tomorrow*	**nunc**	*now*
heri	*yesterday*	**saepe**	*often*
hódie	*today*	**semper**	*always*
non	*not*	**tum**	*then, at that time*
numquam	*never*	**umquam**	*ever*

Latin Sayings

Ora et labora.
semper fidelis
Errare est humanum.

nunc aut numquam
Fortes fortuna juvat.

35

LESSON XIII

ORAL RECITATION/REVIEW
Teacher: *Salvete, amici Latinae*
Students: *Salve, magistra (magister)*
Teacher: *Súrgite*
Teacher: *Recitemus*

    personal endings
    tense endings - 5 tenses
    amo - six tenses, p.p.
    do, sto, juvo, lavo - p.p.
    sum - six tenses, p.p.

Teacher: *Sedete*

Grammar Questions: 1-56

LESSON XIII

UNITS I and II REVIEW

First Conjugation - Indicative Active
amo amare amavi amatus
present stem **ama -**

Present	
am**o**	ama**mus**
ama**s**	ama**tis**
ama**t**	ama**nt**

Imperfect	
ama**bam**	ama**bamus**
ama**bas**	ama**batis**
ama**bat**	ama**bant**

Future	
ama**bo**	amá**bimus**
ama**bis**	amá**bitis**
ama**bit**	ama**bunt**

perfect stem **amav -**

Perfect	
amav**i**	amáv**imus**
amav**isti**	amav**istis**
amav**it**	amav**erunt**

Pluperfect	
amáv**eram**	amav**eramus**
amáv**eras**	amav**eratis**
amáv**erat**	amáv**erant**

Future Perfect	
amáv**ero**	amav**érimus**
amáv**eris**	amav**éritis**
amáv**erit**	amáv**erint**

Sum - Indicative Active
sum esse fui futurus
present stem **--**

Present	
su**m**	su**mus**
e**s**	es**tis**
es**t**	su**nt**

Imperfect	
era**m**	era**mus**
era**s**	era**tis**
era**t**	era**nt**

Future	
er**o**	éri**mus**
eri**s**	éri**tis**
eri**t**	eru**nt**

perfect stem **fu-**

Perfect	
fu**i**	fú**imus**
fu**isti**	fu**istis**
fu**it**	fu**erunt**

Pluperfect	
fú**eram**	fu**eramus**
fú**eras**	fu**eratis**
fú**erat**	fú**erant**

Future Perfect	
fú**ero**	fu**érimus**
fú**eris**	fú**éritis**
fú**erit**	fú**erint**

36

This lesson is for the purpose of review, consolidation, and mastery of vocabulary and conjugations. Make copies of workbook pages to use as drill sheets and practice tests.

MASTERY GOALS FOR GRAMMAR AND VOCABULARY
1) Be able to recite and write the conjugation of the model verb **amo** in all six tenses with meanings.
2) Be able to recite and write the conjugation of any 1st conjugation verb in all six tenses with meanings.
3) Be able to recite and write the conjugation of **sum** in all six tenses with meanings.
4) Be able to translate and spell correctly 50 verbs and 10 adverbs, Latin to English and English to Latin.
5) Be able to recite and write the principal parts of each regular Latin verb.
6) Be able to recite and write the irregular principal parts of **do**, **sto**, **lavo**, **juvo** and the irregular verb **sum**.
7) Be able to give a synopsis of any verb in any person and number in all six tenses.
8) Form drill mastery. Rapid translation of inflected forms from Latin to English and English to Latin.
9) Know Latin Sayings - Latin to English and English to Latin.

See Teacher Guidelines for Games and Review Activities.

There is a test for this unit.

Verbs

accuso	to accuse	hábito	to live in, dwell	paro	to prepare
adoro	to adore	júdico	to judge	perturbo	to disturb
ámbulo	to walk	juvo	to help	porto	to carry
amo	to love, like	laboro	to work	pugno	to fight
appello	to address	laudo	to praise	puto	to think
aro	to plow	lavo	to wash	rogo	to ask
celo	to hide	líbero	to set free	saluto	to greet
clamo	to shout	muto	to change	servo	to guard, keep
creo	to create	narro	to tell	specto	to look at
culpo	to blame	nato	to swim	spero	to hope
delecto	to delight, please	návigo	to sail	sto	to stand
demonstro	to show, point out	nego	to deny	súpero	to overcome, surpass
do	to give	núntio	to report	tempto	to tempt
dúbito	to doubt	óccupo	to seize	voco	to call
erro	to err, wander	oppugno	to attack	volo	to fly
exploro	to explore	opto	to desire, wish	vúlnero	to wound
exspecto	to wait for, expect	oro	to speak, pray	sum	to be

Adverbs

cras	tomorrow	nunc	now
heri	yesterday	saepe	often
hódie	today	semper	always
non	not	tum	then, at that time
numquam	never	umquam	ever

Latin Sayings

Ora et labora.
Stabat Mater
In umbra, ígitur, pugnábimus.
In choro recitémus.
Errare est humanum.

Civis Romanus sum.
nunc aut numquam
semper fidelis
Fortes fortuna juvat.

37

MILESTONE MARKER 2

Congratulations. You have reached another important milestone in your study of Latin. Being able to conjugate regular and irregular 1st conjugation verbs and sum in all six tenses is a huge accomplishment that you have achieved in only (13 ?) short weeks. There are many people who study Latin for years that cannot conjugate these verbs nearly as well as you! Now that you have learned how verbs work, you will be able to learn the other three conjugations in half the time. Look at Unit V. You will learn the Second Conjugation in only six lessons instead of the 13 it took for the 1st Conjugation. You are well on your way to becoming a Latin scholar.

Now we will turn to that other very important part of speech, nouns.

UNIT III INTRODUCTION

The purpose of the Unit Introductions is to give you and your students an overview of the content of the unit. You are not expected to understand all of the concepts, but it is helpful to have a quick introduction of terms and ideas that the students will be encountering.

The Unit Introduction also helps students to see the big picture, to see each lesson as part of a whole that all fits together. Learning is a journey. To look back at where you have been and look forward to where you are going motivates students and gives encouragement for the work ahead.

GRAMMAR - CHALK TALK
Ask students to read over this page silently.

Latin is a language of what?
(stems and endings)

Families of verbs are called what?
(conjugations) What do the endings of verbs tell you? (person, number, tense, voice, and mood)

Families of nouns are called what?
(declensions) What are the four attributes of nouns? (declension, gender, number, and case)

UNIT III INTRODUCTION

♦ Just as verbs are divided into four families called conjugations, nouns are grouped into five families called *declensions*.

♦ There are four attributes of nouns:

declension	1st, 2nd, 3rd, 4th, 5th
gender	masculine, feminine, neuter
number	singular and plural
case	nominative, genitive, dative, accusative, ablative

♦ Nouns that name male or female persons, such as *father* or *queen,* are masculine or feminine and have *natural* (real) *gender*. Nouns that name non-living things have *grammatical gender* and are identified as masculine, feminine, or neuter.

♦ Case refers to the job (function) of a noun in a sentence. (See the Appendix, pages 102-104) Learn these quick uses for the Latin cases.

nominative	the *subject* case	the rose
genitive	the *possessive* or *of* case	of the rose
dative	the *indirect object* or *to/for* case	to the rose
accusative	the *direct object* case	the rose
ablative	the *in/by/with/from* case	in the rose

♦ The 1st and 2nd declension nouns and adjectives are similar and will be studied together. The 3rd-5th Declensions will be studied in Unit 4.

♦ In Latin vocabulary lists and dictionaries, the nominative singular form is followed by the genitive singular ending and the gender. This is a listing for *rose* in a Latin dictionary or vocabulary list.

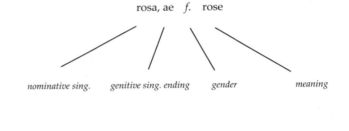

rosa, ae *f.* rose

nominative sing.   genitive sing. ending   gender   meaning

38

How many declensions are there? (5) Name them. (1st, 2nd, 3rd, 4th, 5th)
How many genders are there? (3) Name them. (masculine, feminine, neuter)
Nouns that name male or female living things have what kind of gender? (natural gender)
Nouns that name non-living things have what kind of gender? (grammatical gender)
How many grammar numbers are there? (2) Name them. (singular and plural)
How many cases are there? (5) Name them. (nominative, genitive, dative, accusative, ablative)
Recite names of cases *in choro* several times. Have a few students recite names of cases individually.
What does the word *case* mean in grammar? (the job (function) of a noun in a sentence)

Write the names of the cases on the board as you ask these questions. What is the subject case? (nominative) The possessive case? (genitive) The indirect object case? (dative) The direct object case? (accusative) The in/by/with/from case? (ablative) Go over the spellings. (Students frequently misspell *genitive* as *genative.*) Students must memorize cases in order. Use the *Disappearing Line Technique* and the acronym NGDAA. *Never Gag Down An Ant. No Good Dogs Are Around* (Or let students compete to make up one for your class).

Write the dictionary entry of **rosa** on the board as shown in the last bullet.
What case is used for the dictionary entry? (nominative)
What follows the dictionary entry? (genitive singular ending, gender, and meaning)

UNIT III

1st and 2nd Declension Nouns and Adjectives

A Relief from the Arch of Titus

Spoils taken from the Temple of Jerusalem in the Jewish War—depicted on the Arch of Titus on the Via Sacra in the Forum Romanum. The arch, commemorating the sack of Jerusalem in AD 70, clearly shows the Roman soldiers carrying the seven-candlestick menorah in a victory procession. For Americans today this is one of the most meaningful and poignant sights in the ancient Forum.

39

Cases. The concept of <u>case</u> is difficult for students. If you need additional help in understanding case, see pages 102-104 of the text appendix. For students in 5th grade and up, you may give the following explanation if you like or you may omit it. Students will not completely understand, but that is OK. Write the following sentence on the board, ask students which words are nouns, and underline them:

<u>**Mark's friend**</u> gave <u>**Lucy**</u> a <u>**rose**</u> in the <u>**garden**</u>.

There are five nouns with five different jobs to do. What is the subject? (*friend*) What is the subject case in Latin? (nominative) What is the direct object? (*rose*) What is the direct object case in Latin? (accusative) What noun shows possession? (*Mark's*) What is the possessive case in Latin? (genitive) What noun is the indirect object? (*Lucy*) What is the indirect object case in Latin? (dative) What noun is the object of a preposition? (*garden*) What is the *in/by/with/from* case in Latin? (ablative)

WORKBOOK NOTE: Complete the Unit Introduction page for Lesson 14 in your workbook.

LESSON XIV

1 **ORAL RECITATION/REVIEW**
Greeting
Teacher: *Recitemus*
> **personal & tense endings**
> **amo** - six tenses, p.p.
> **do, sto, juvo, lavo** - p.p.
> **sum** - six tenses, p.p.

Grammar Review Questions: 1-71

2 **LATIN SAYING**
Say aloud and ask students to repeat after you.

Roma -ae *f.*	Rome
aeternus -a -um *adj.*	eternal

4 **GRAMMAR - CHALK TALK**
First Declension. Latin is a language of? (stems and endings) What are the four attributes of nouns? (declension, gender, number and case) What is the stem? (the part of the word that doesn't change) Look at the declension chart. What is the stem of mensa? **(mens)** Write **mens** on the board 10 times and ask a student for the singular endings

---

Roma Aeterna   *Eternal Rome*

First Declension

Case	Singular	Ending	Plural	Ending
nominative	mens**a**	-a	mens**ae**	-ae
genitive	mens**ae**	-ae	mens**arum**	-arum
dative	mens**ae**	-ae	mens**is**	-is
accusative	mens**am**	-am	mens**as**	-as
ablative	mens**ā**	-ā	mens**is**	-is

◆ **Mensa** is the model noun chosen to illustrate the *1st Declension*. The stem of **mensa** is **mens**. Drop the nominative singular ending **a** to find the stem.[4] To *decline* a noun, add the *case endings* to the stem.

◆ The ablative singular ending of 1st declension nouns will be marked with a *macron* in this text to distinguish it from the nominative singular ending.[5]

◆ In English, the words **the**, **a**, and **an** are called *articles*. There are no *articles* in Latin. **Mensa** may be translated three ways: **table, a table, the table.**

◆ All nouns whose *genitive singular* ends in **ae** belong to the 1st Declension.

Vocabulary

Latin	Gender	English	Derivative
agrícola -ae	*m.*	farmer	*agriculture*
Itália -ae	*f.*	Italy	
Maria -ae	*f.*	Mary	
mensa -ae	*f.*	table	*mesa*
nauta -ae	*m.*	sailor	*nautical*
poeta -ae	*m.*	poet	
puella -ae	*f.*	girl	
regina -ae	*f.*	queen	
Roma -ae	*f.*	Rome	
terra -ae	*f.*	earth, land	*territory*

*Oral Drill for Lesson XIV is on page 112.

40

---

and then for the plural and write each on the board. Which cases have the same endings? (genitive singular, dative singular and nominative plural, and dative and ablative plural) What is different about the ablative singular form? (It is marked with a macron to distinguish it from the nominative singular.)

> ****Memorize the declension of *mensa*, the 1st declension case endings, and the 5 cases in order.****

Use the *Disappearing Line Technique* as described in the Teaching Guidelines.

Articles. English, Greek, German, Spanish, French, and many other languages have articles. Look at **Bullet 3** and give the English articles. (*the, a, an*) What is the difference between *a* and *an*? (*a* is used before nouns that begin with consonants, *an* is used before nouns that begin with vowels) *A* and *an* are the indefinite articles, referring to something in general, and *the* is the definite article, referring to a particular thing. *I ate a banana. I ate the banana.* Articles are useful because they signify that the words that follow them are being used as nouns.

Word Study ◆ Grammar ◆ Syntax

- ◆ Every Latin noun has *gender*. There are three genders: *masculine, feminine and neuter,* identified by the abbreviations **m.**, **f.**, **n.**

- ◆ 1st declension nouns are usually *feminine*, even when they name non-living things like **mensa, Italia, terra** and **Roma.**

- ◆ Some nouns have *natural gender* in addition to their *grammar* gender. **Maria, puella,** and **regina** name female persons so they are feminine by nature.

- ◆ However, **nauta, agricola,** and **poeta** are masculine by nature because they name male persons. (In the Roman world these occupations were always male.) If the natural gender and grammar gender are different, natural gender always wins.

- ◆ Here are two gender rules to remember with their abbreviations.
  1) NG. Natural Gender. Nouns that name male persons are masculine and nouns that name female persons are feminine. Natural gender *trumps* all other gender rules.
  2) 1D F. 1st declension nouns are usually feminine.

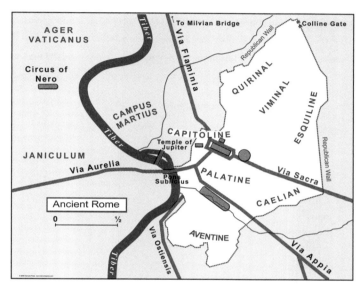

The Seven Hills of Rome

41

VOCABULARY –

Say each noun aloud with its complete genitive form (mensa, mensae) and meaning. Have students repeat after you.

Pronunciation helps:
s as in *sing*
au as in *out*
o and **e** in **poeta** pronounced separately

Derivatives:
   terrestrial
   extraterrestrial
   terrain
   Mediterranean
   nautilus

Gender. What are the two genders in the natural world? (male and female; neuter indicates no gender) What terms are used for male and female genders in grammar? (masculine and feminine) Write words on board and note spelling. When learning nouns in Latin, Greek, German, Spanish, French, and many other languages, you must also learn the gender of the noun. Ask students for some examples. (See grammar appendix in text, page 105) In these languages, nouns that refer to non-living things often have grammatical gender and can be masculine or feminine.

Which vocabulary words name non-living things and have grammatical gender? (**mensa, terra, Roma,** and **Itália**) What is their gender and why? (They are feminine because 1st declension nouns are usually feminine.) What kind of gender do they have? (grammatical gender)

Why are **puella, Maria,** and **regina** feminine? (because they name female persons) Why are **poeta, agrícola,** and **nauta** masculine? (because they name male persons) What kind of gender do these nouns have? (natural gender)

What is the first gender rule that always applies regardless of declension? (**NG** - The natural gender rule. Nouns that name male persons are masculine; nouns that name female persons are feminine. Natural gender trumps all other rules.) What is the 1st declension gender rule? (**1D F** - 1st declension nouns are usually feminine.)

LESSON XV

① ORAL RECITATION/REVIEW
Greeting
Teacher: *Recitemus*

    personal & tense endings
    1st conj. p.p. endings
    amo - six tenses, p.p.
    do, sto, juvo, lavo - p.p.
    sum - six tenses, p.p.
    case names
    mensa, ae

Grammar Review Questions: 1-76

② LATIN SAYING
Say aloud and ask students to repeat after you.

annus -i *m.*	year
anno *abl. case*	
dóminus -i *m.*	lord, master
dómini *gen. case*	

In Latin *case* often takes the place of prepositions. **Anno Dómini** is a good illustration of this syntax principle.
Anno - in the year
Domini - of the Lord

④ GRAMMAR - CHALK TALK
How many declensions are there? (5) This is the second declension and we will know them all in no time! What is the stem of **servus**? (**serv**) Recite the declension of **servus** for students

---

LESSON XV

Anno Dómini (A.D.)   *In the year of our Lord*

Second Declension Masculine

Case	Singular	Ending	Plural	Ending
nominative	serv**us**	-us	serv**i**	-i
genitive	serv**i**	-i	serv**orum**	-orum
dative	serv**o**	-o	serv**is**	-is
accusative	serv**um**	-um	serv**os**	-os
ablative	serv**o**	-o	serv**is**	-is

♦ **Servus** is the model noun chosen to illustrate *2nd Declension* nouns ending in **us**.

♦ The stem is **serv**. For these nouns, drop the nominative singular ending **us** to find the stem.[4]

♦ 2nd declension nouns that end in **us** in the nominative singular are usually **masculine**.

♦ **Deus** and **Dominus** are capitalized when referring to *Jesus* or *God*. Use lower case when referring to pagan gods.

Vocabulary

Latin	Gender	English	Derivative
agnus -i	*m.*	lamb	*St. Agnes*
amicus -i	*m.*	friend	*amicable*
annus -i	*m.*	year	*annual*
Christus -i	*m.*	Christ	
deus -i	*m.*	god	*deity*
dóminus -i	*m.*	lord, master	*dominate*
equus -i	*m.*	horse	*equine*
fílius -i	*m.*	son	*filial*
mundus -i	*m.*	world, mankind	*mundane*
servus -i	*m.*	slave, servant	*servile*

42

---

and then have students recite *in choro* several times. Ask students for the 1st declension endings and write on the board. Ask students for the 2nd declension endings and write next to them. Compare and contrast case endings. The characteristic vowel for the 1st declension is the letter **a**, and for the 2nd declension it is the letter **o**.

	mensa	**servus**
Genitive s. and nominative pl. endings are the same	ae	i
Accusative s. ends in letter **m**	am	um
accusative pl. is similar	as	os
abl. singular is declension vowel	a	o
gen. pl. is similar	arum	orum
dat. and abl. plural endings are **is**	is	is

        Memorize the declension of *servus* and the 2nd declension masculine case endings.

Use the *Disappearing Line Technique* as described in the Teaching Guidelines.

DERIVATIVES NOTE: *Agnes* is technically not a derivative of **agnus**, but the two words became associated.

Word Study ◆ Grammar ◆ Syntax

◆ The subject of a verb is in the nominative case. To form a plural subject, use the plural nominative case ending, **i** for 2nd decl. **us** nouns, and **ae** for 1st declension nouns.

◆ Here is a third gender rule.
  (3) **2D us M**: 2nd declension **us** nouns are usually masculine.

◆ English words that show their 1st/2nd declension origin by retaining the Latin plural endings are:

alumna, alumnae	*formula, formulae*	*fungus, fungi*
alumnus, alumni	*cactus, cacti*	

Anno Dómini. The dating system based on the birth of Christ was developed in the Middle Ages. *B.C.* stands for the English *Before Christ*. *A.D.* stands for the Latin **Anno Dómini**, which means *in the year of Our Lord*. *A.D.* refers to a year following the birth of Christ, and does not mean *after death*.

Oral Drill - Nominative Case

year	1. annus		1. horse	equus	
world	2. mundus		2. son	fílius	
friends	3. amici		3. gods	dei	
horses	4. equi		4. lambs	agni	
lamb	5. agnus		5. friend	amicus	
sons	6. fílii		6. worlds	mundi	
slaves	7. servi		7. years	anni	
masters	8. dómini		8. servant	servus	
Christ	9. Christus		9. lord	dóminus	
god	10. deus		10. Christ	Christus	

43

VOCABULARY ③

Say each noun aloud with its genitive form and meaning. Have students repeat after you.

What is the genitive singular ending of these nouns? (**i**) What is the gender? (masculine) Which nouns have natural gender? (**Christus, dóminus, fílius, deus**)

Which have grammatical gender? (**annus, mundus**)

(**agnus, equus, servus, deus, amicus**) Animals and other nouns can be either gender and thus may have masculine and feminine forms (**amicus, amica, deus, dea (goddess)**, etc.)

Pronunciation helps:
c is hard before **a**, **o**, **u** and soft before **e**, **i**, **ae**. amic<u>u</u>s, amic<u>i</u>
gn = /ny/ as in lasagna, canyon
qu = kw. There is only one **u** sound in **equus**.

Derivatives:
  service
  annals, anniversary
  dominion
  equestrian
  deify

GRAMMAR - CHALK TALK

Write the names of the cases on the board. Ask students for the *job* of each case and write on the board.

nominative case	*subject* case
genitive case	*possessive* or *of* case
dative case	*indirect object* or *to/for* case
accusative case	*direct object* case
ablative case	*in/by/with/from* case

How do we show possession in English? (two ways, by an **apostrophe** or an *of* expression)
the voice of God, God's voice

How do we show an indirect object in English? (two ways, **word order** or a *to/for* expression) (English grammars will identify *to him* as a prepositional phrase rather than an indirect object. But for the purposes of translating into Latin, it is an indirect object.)
I gave **him** a book, I gave a book **to him**

The ablative case is often used in place of what prepositions? (*in, by, with, from*)
Memorize the jobs of each case.

① ORAL RECITATION/REVIEW
Greeting
Teacher: *Recitemus*

> **personal & tense endings**
> **1st conj. p.p. endings**
> **amo** - six tenses, p.p.
> **do, sto, juvo, lavo** - p.p.
> **sum** - six tenses, p.p.
> **case names**
> **mensa, ae**
> **servus, i**

Grammar Review Questions: 1-78

② LATIN SAYING
Say aloud and ask students to repeat after you.

ante *prep. with acc.*   before
(In Latin the object of a preposition
is either in the abl. or acc. case.)
bellum -i *n.*   war

Teach the anglicized pronunciation of
this saying (an tee bell um) because
that is what students will hear.

---

ante bellum   *before the war*

Second Declension Neuter

Case	Singular	Ending	Plural	Ending
nominative	bell um	-um	bell a	-a
genitive	bell i	-i	bell orum	-orum
dative	bell o	-o	bell is	-is
accusative	bell um	-um	bell a	-a
ablative	bell o	-o	bell is	-is

♦ **Bellum** is the model noun chosen to illustrate 2nd declension nouns ending in **um**. The stem is **bell**. For these nouns, drop the nominative singular ending **um** to find the stem.[4]

♦ The 2nd declension has two subgroups: 1) nouns that end in **us** in the nominative singular and are usually masculine 2) nouns that end in **um** in the nominative singular and are **neuter** (*n*).

> All nouns whose genitive singular ends in **i** belong to the 2nd Declension.

Vocabulary

bellum -i	*n.*	war	*bellicose*
caelum -i	*n.*[6]	sky, heaven	*celestial*
débitum -i	*n.*	debt, sin	*debit*
donum -i	*n.*	gift	*donation*
forum -i	*n.*	forum, marketplace	*forum*
óppidum -i	*n.*	town	
regnum -i	*n.*	kingdom	*reign*
saxum -i	*n.*	rock	
templum -i	*n.*	temple	
verbum -i	*n.*	word	*verb, verbal*

44

---

④ GRAMMAR - CHALK TALK

How many declensions are there? (5) Although there are five declensions, you will have seven paradigms (models) to learn because both the second and third declensions have two subgroups. No problem, though! We will still learn them in no time!

What is the stem of **bellum**? (**bell**) Write on the board ten times and ask for the singular and then the plural endings and write on board. Let's make some observations. What is the most distinctive thing about this set of case endings? (nominative and accusative endings are same in both singular and plural) Why is this a problem? (You can't tell the subject from the direct object by the case ending!) What is really troublesome about the plural endings? (nominative and accusative cases end in the letter **a**) What does the case ending **a** mean in the 1st declension? (singular nominative or ablative - with macron)

Write the case endings for **servus** on the board. Compare and contrast these two sets of endings. Write the case endings for the 1st declension on the board and again compare and contrast.

Memorize the declension of *bellum* and the 2nd declension neuter case endings.

Word Study ◆ Grammar ◆ Syntax

◆ There are neuter nouns in the 2nd, 3rd, and 4th declensions. All neuter nouns obey the *neuter rule*:

the nominative and accusative case forms are identical
the nominative and accusative plural case ending is -a

◆ Here is a fourth gender rule.
(4) **2D um N**: 2nd declension nouns that end in **um** are neuter.

◆ As you learn the 5 declensions you will see that a particular ending can indicate different cases in different declensions. The letter **a** is the nominative singular ending in the 1st declension, but it is the nominative and accusative plural ending in the 2nd declension neuter.

◆ English words that show their 2nd declension neuter origin by retaining the Latin plural endings are:

datum, data	medium, media	bacterium, bacteria
curriculum, curricula	stratum, strata	memorandum, memoranda

Ante bellum refers to the unique culture of a landed aristocracy that existed in the American South before the Civil War.

Oral Drill - Nominative Case

poet	1. **poeta**		1. gift	donum	
sailor	2. **nauta**		2. gifts	dona	
wars	3. **bella**		3. wars	bella	
words	4. **verba**		4. war	bellum	
debts	5. **debita**		5. towns	óppida	
gifts	6. **dona**		6. town	óppidum	
girl	7. **puella**		7. kingdom	regnum	
towns	8. **óppida**		8. kingdoms	regna	
land	9. **terra**		9. word	verbum	
rocks	10. **saxa**		10. words	verba	

45

VOCABULARY
Say each noun aloud with its genitive form and meaning. Have students repeat after you.

All vocabulary words end in what two letters? (**um**) And are what gender? (neuter) How do you know these words are 2nd declension? (the genitive singular is **i**)

Pronunciation helps:
c is soft before **e, i, ae**, and has the sound of /**ch**/
gn = /**ny**/ as in *lasagna, canyon*

Derivatives:
belligerent, rebel
donate, donor
verbal, verbose, adverb
debt

GRAMMAR - CHALK TALK
Learn the neuter rule and the 4th gender rule. (**Bullets 3** and **4**)

The English words that have Latin plural endings will help students remember the **a** plural ending for the neuter nouns. (**Bullets 5** and **6**).

LESSON XVII

1 ORAL RECITATION/REVIEW
Greeting
Teacher: *Recitemus*

    personal & tense endings
    1st conj. p.p. endings
    amo - six tenses, p.p.
    do, sto, juvo, lavo - p.p.
    sum - six tenses, p.p.
    case names
    mensa, ae
    servus, i
    bellum, i

Grammar Review Questions: 1-84

First and Second Declensions

Case	1st Declension S.	1st Declension Pl.	2nd Declension Masculine S.	2nd Declension Masculine Pl.	2nd Declension Neuter S.	2nd Declension Neuter Pl.
nom.	mens**a**	mens**ae**	serv**us**	serv**i**	bell**um**	bell**a**
gen.	mens**ae**	mens**arum**	serv**i**	serv**orum**	bell**i**	bell**orum**
dat.	mens**ae**	mens**is**	serv**o**	serv**is**	bell**o**	bell**is**
acc.	mens**am**	mens**as**	serv**um**	serv**os**	bell**um**	bell**a**
abl.	mens**ā**	mens**is**	serv**o**	serv**is**	bell**o**	bell**is**

◆ The 1st and 2nd declensions can be considered a unit because they include all three genders and have similar case endings.

Vocabulary Review

agnus -i m.	*lamb*		**Maria -ae f.**	*Mary*
agrícola -ae m.	*farmer*		**mensa -ae f.**	*table*
amicus -i m.	*friend*		**mundus -i m.**	*world, mankind*
annus -i m.	*year*		**nauta -ae m.**	*sailor*
bellum -i n.	*war*		**óppidum -i n.**	*town*
caelum -i n.	*sky, heaven*		**poeta -ae m.**	*poet*
Christus -i m.	*Christ*		**puella -ae f.**	*girl*
débitum -i n.	*debt, sin*		**regina -ae f.**	*queen*
deus -i m.	*god*		**regnum -i n.**	*kingdom*
dóminus -i m.	*lord, master*		**Roma -ae f.**	*Rome*
donum -i n.	*gift*		**saxum -i n.**	*rock*
equus -i m.	*horse*		**servus -i m.**	*slave, servant*
fílius -i m.	*son*		**templum -i n.**	*temple*
forum -i n.	*forum, marketplace*		**terra -ae f.**	*earth, land*
Itália -ae f.	*Italy*		**verbum -i n.**	*word*

46

2 GRAMMAR - CHALK TALK

This lesson and the three following, Lessons 16-18, are a time to solidify mastery of the 1st and 2nd declensions. Students cannot successfully learn the 3-5th declensions while still struggling with the first two. Overlearning is important in Latin.

The 1st and 2nd declensions are a unit in which you have all three genders and many similarities in case endings. Ask students to help you list these similarities.

    m in the accusative singular
    the characteristic vowel of each declension in the ablative singular, **a** or **o**
    arum or **orum** in the genitive plural
    is in the dative and ablative plural

Word Study ♦ Grammar ♦ Syntax

♦ Because the nominative singular is variable in most declensions, the genitive singular is used to classify nouns.

> If the genitive singular ends in **-ae** the noun is 1st declension.
> If the genitive singular ends in **-i** the noun is 2nd declension.

♦ English names often correspond to the Latin masculine and feminine endings.
   Julius/Julia   Cornelius/Cornelia   Marius/Maria   Marcus/Marcia

♦ **Subject-verb Agreement**. If the subject of the verb is a noun, the 3rd person form of the verb is used. The subject and verb must agree in person and number. A singular subject takes a singular verb; a plural subject takes a plural verb. This is *Sentence Pattern #1* on pages 95-96.

Singular: Plural:
Servus laborat. *The servant (he) works.*   **Servi laborant**. *The servants (they) work.*

Oral Drill - Nominative Case

lands	1. **terrae**		1. kingdoms	regna
years	2. **anni**		2. world	mundus
queen	3. **regina**		3. temples	templa
words	4. **verba**		4. poets	poetae
horse	5. **equus**		5. friends	amici
sailors	6. **nautae**		6. debts	débita
rock	7. **saxum**		7. heaven	caelum
lamb	8. **agnus**		8. wars	bella
sons	9. **filii**		9. girl	puella
gifts	10. **dona**		10. servants	servi

47

MASTERY GOALS FOR GRAMMAR AND VOCABULARY
Students should be able to:
1) Spell all thirty nouns correctly and give the genitive singular, gender, and declension of each noun, going from Latin to English and English to Latin.
2) Decline three model nouns: **mensa, servus, bellum**
3) Decline any of the thirty nouns correctly.
4) Know and be able to apply the four gender rules.
5) Write the five cases in order and spell correctly. Know the *job* of each case.

LESSON XVIII

1 ORAL RECITATION/REVIEW
Greeting
Teacher: *Recitemus*

> **personal & tense endings**
> **1st conj. p.p. endings**
> **amo** - six tenses, p.p.
> **do, sto, juvo, lavo** - p.p.
> **sum** - six tenses, p.p.
> **case names**
> **mensa, ae**
> **servus, i**
> **bellum, i**

Grammar Review Questions: 1-84

2 LATIN SAYING

mater matris *f.*	mother
Itália -ae *f.*	Italy
Itáliae *gen. case*	
Roma -ae *f.*	Rome

The mother of Italy is Rome. Latin often omits linking verbs that are obvious.

4 GRAMMAR - CHALK TALK

There is actually nothing new to learn in this grammar chart. The declension of **bonus** has the same case endings that you have already learned. The difficulty is in the concept of **agreement**, that an adjective can be written 18 different ways so that it **agrees** with its noun. There is nothing like this in English. Latin stretches the mind.

Mater Itáliae Roma.   *The mother of Italy, Rome.*

First and Second Declension Adjectives

Case	Singular			Plural		
	M.	F.	N.	M.	F.	N.
nom.	bon**us**	bon**a**	bon**um**	bon**i**	bon**ae**	bon**a**
gen.	bon**i**	bon**ae**	bon**i**	bon**orum**	bon**arum**	bon**orum**
dat.	bon**o**	bon**ae**	bon**o**	bon**is**	bon**is**	bon**is**
acc.	bon**um**	bon**am**	bon**um**	bon**os**	bon**as**	bon**a**
abl.	bon**o**	bon**ā**	bon**o**	bon**is**	bon**is**	bon**is**

♦ An adjective modifies or describes a noun or pronoun. In Latin there are adjectives that are declined in all three genders with endings identical to the nouns of the 1st and 2nd declensions. They are called *1st/2nd Declension Adjectives.*

♦ In dictionary form, the adjective is given in its masculine form, followed by the feminine and neuter nominative singular endings.

Vocabulary

aeternus -a -um	eternal, everlasting	*eternity*
altus -a -um	high, deep	*altitude*
bonus -a -um	good	*bonus*
latus -a -um	wide, broad	*latitude*
magnus -a -um	great, large	*magnify*
malus -a -um	bad	*malice*
multus -a -um	much (pl. many)	*multitude*
novus -a -um	new	*novelty, novel*
parvus -a -um	small	
sanctus -a -um	sacred, holy	*sanctify*

*Oral Drill for Lesson XVIII is on page 112.

48

ways so that it **agrees** with its noun. There is nothing like this in English. Latin stretches the mind.

What is an adjective? (a word that modifies or describes a noun or a pronoun) What three sets of endings do you see in this chart? (the same endings of the 1st and 2nd declensions which correspond to masculine, feminine, and neuter nouns) It is helpful to think of the 1st and 2nd declensions as a unit. Students have learned to recite each declension individually, singular column and then plural column. With adjectives it is customary to start reciting the same endings in horizontal rows for each case. Example: **bonus, bona, bonum, boni, bonae, boni, bono, bonae, bono**, etc. This is awkward at first but is good practice for students and helps when they learn the 3rd person pronouns and other pronouns which are recited the same way.
Agreement. What is the rule in **Bullets 4, 5**? (An adjective agrees with its noun in gender, number, and case, but not declension.)
Write **puella bona** on the board. What is the gender, number, and case of **puella**? (feminine, singular, nominative) Of **bona**? (feminine, singular, nominative) Do they agree in gender, number, and case? (Yes) What does **puella bona** mean? (*good girl*)

Write **puellarum bonarum** on the board. What is the gender, number, and case of **puellarum**? (feminine, plural, genitive) Of **bonarum**? (feminine, plural, genitive) Do they agree in gender, number, and case? (Yes) What does **puellarum bonarum** mean? (*of the good girls*)

Word Study ◆ Grammar ◆ Syntax

◆ In Latin, adjectives may precede or follow their nouns. Though not a strict rule, adjectives of quantity or size often precede nouns, and adjectives of quality often follow nouns. Some adjectives such as *magnus*, *altus*, and *latus* can refer to either quantity or quality depending on the context.

◆ In Latin, an adjective must agree with its noun in gender, number, and case,

puell**a** bon**a**	serv**us** bon**us**	oppid**um** bon**um**
good girl	*good servant*	*good town*

but not declension. The three 1st declension masculine nouns, **agricola**, **poeta**, and **nauta**, are modified by the 2nd declension masculine adjective forms.

agricol**a** bon**us**	agricol**ae** bon**i**
good farmer	*good farmers*

Mater Italiae Roma. Through conquest, the language and culture of Rome united Italy and the whole Mediterranean world, and thus Rome gave birth not only to Italy but to Western Civilization. This saying is from the Roman historian, Florus.

49

VOCABULARY
*Say each adjective in horizontal rows (**bonus, bona, bonum**, etc.). Have students repeat after you.*

In a dictionary or vocabulary list, the entry letters that follow a Latin noun are what? (the genitive singular ending) Folliong a Latin verb? (the infinitive ending) What follows an adjective entry? (the feminine and neuter nominative singular endings)

What is the opposite of **bonus**? (**malus**) **Magnus**? (**parvus**) **Altus**? (**latus**). **Novus** and **aeternus** are not opposites, but close.

Pronunciation helps:
aeternus - ae = ay, er = air
sanctus = sahnk toos

Derivatives:
> *bonanza, bonbon, bonny*
> *malicious, malady*
> *maladjusted, dismal*
> *magnification, magnum*
> *novel, novice, innovate*
> *altimeter*
> *multiply*
> *sanctification, sanctuary*

GRAMMAR - CHALK TALK
Do you think that the endings of the noun and the adjective will always be the same if they must agree in gender, number, and case? When will they not be the same? (when writing an adjective for the three 1st declension nouns that are masculine) Write **agricola bona** on the board. Ask for the gender, number, and case of **bona** (feminine, singular, nominative) and **agricola** (masculine, singular, nominative).

How should we write *the good farmer* in Latin?   **agricola bonus** Now they agree in gender, number, and case.

What do you think will happen when you have nouns from declensions 3-5?

Word Order. Look at **Bullet 3**.
Write on board: **novum templum**   and   **templum novum**
Both mean the same in Latin. What is the general rule for adjective word order?
(*Usually*, adjectives of quantity or size precede their nouns, and adjectives of quality follow the noun.)

Go through the vocabulary list and identify adjectives of quantity or size (**parvus, multus, latus**) and quality (**bonus, malus, novus, aeternus, sanctus**). Some can be either quantity or quality: **magnus, altus.**

LESSON XIX

① ORAL RECITATION/REVIEW
Greeting
Teacher: *Recitemus*

> **personal & tense endings**
> **1st conj. p.p. endings**
> **amo** - six tenses, p.p.
> **do, sto, juvo, lavo,** p.p.
> **sum** - six tenses, p.p.
> **case names**
> **mensa, ae**
> **servus, i**
> **bellum, i**
> **bonus, bona, bonum**

Grammar Review Questions: 1-88

② LATIN SAYING
Say aloud and ask students to repeat after you.

quáttuor	four
indeclinable adj.	
annus -i *m.*	year
anni *gen. sing.*	
tempus témporis *n.*	time
témpora *nom. pl.*	

The literal translation is
four times of the year.

LESSON XIX

Quáttuor anni témpora   *The four seasons of the year*

Numbers 1 - 10

		Cardinal			Ordinal	
I		**unus -a -um**	one		**primus -a -um**	first
II		**duo**	two		**secundus -a -um**	second
III		**tres**	three		**tértius -a -um**	third
IV		**quáttuor**	four		**quartus -a -um**	fourth
V		**quinque**	five		**quintus -a -um**	fifth
VI		**sex**	six		**sextus -a -um**	sixth
VII		**septem**	seven		**séptimus -a -um**	seventh
VIII		**octo**	eight		**octavus -a -um**	eighth
IX		**novem**	nine		**nonus -a -um**	ninth
X		**decem**	ten		**décimus -a -um**	tenth

♦ **Cardinal** means most important. Cardinal numbers are counting numbers. The cardinal numbers are a special type of adjective. The numbers **four-ten** are indeclinable. **Unus, duo,** and **tres** are declinable but will not be declined in this text because they have irregularities in some cases.[7]

♦ **Ordinal** numbers order things in a series. The ordinal numbers are regular 1st-2nd declension adjectives.

50

④ GRAMMAR - CHALK TALK
What is one definition of *cardinal*? (most important) These are the counting numbers that children learn first. The first three cardinal numbers are declinable, the rest are indeclinable. Derivatives make these numbers easy to remember. Write numbers on the board and, omitting the gender endings for **unus**, recite the cardinal numbers *in choro* several times and then memorize using the *Disappearing Line Technique*.

Class practice: Write numbers in order from memory. Be sure to spell them correctly.

What do *ordinal* numbers do? (order things in a series) All of the ordinal numbers are regular 1st/2nd declension adjectives. Write numbers on the board, omitting the gender endings. Recite *in choro* several times and then memorize, using the *Disappearing Line Technique*.

Class practice: Write ordinal numbers in order from memory. Be sure to spell them correctly.

FYI **Unus -a -um,** and **duo duae duo,** and **tres tria** are all declined. **Unus** and **duo** are irregular in some cases and **tres** is a 3rd declension adjective. These numbers will be used in limited cases in this text.

Memorize cardinal and ordinal numbers in order.

Word Study ◆ Grammar ◆ Syntax

- The *to be* verb, **sum**, shows existence not action. It is usually a *linking verb*, and <u>never</u> takes a direct object.

- A sentence is divided into two main parts: the *subject* and the *predicate*. The subject is **who** or **what** the sentence is about. The predicate contains the verb and tells something about the subject.

- A *predicate adjective* is an adjective that follows a linking verb, describes the subject, and is in the nominative case. See *Sentence Pattern #3*, page 98.

Puella est bona.   **Puellae sunt bonae.**
The girl is good.   *The girls are good.*

- A *predicate nominative* is a noun that follows a linking verb, renames the subject, and is in the nominative case. See *Sentence Pattern #4*, page 98.

Marcus est agrícola.   **Christus est Dóminus.**   **Puellae erunt reginae.**
Mark is a farmer.   Christ is Lord.   The girls will be queens.

> **Quáttuor anni témpora**   The Romans recognized four seasons, as we do.

Oral Drill - Nominative Case

seven kingdoms	1. **septem regna**	1. eight horses	octo equi
first son	2. **primus fílius**	2. the ninth girl	nona puella
nine lambs	3. **novem agni**	3. six sailors	sex nautae
second word	4. **secundum verbum**	4. the eighth queen	octava regina
five gifts	5. **quinque dona**	5. the third town	tértium óppidum
ten years	6. **decem anni**	6. five rocks	quinque saxa
tenth year	7. **décimus annus**	7. the seventh word	séptimum verbum
sixth girl	8. **sexta puella**	8. the fourth farmer	quartus agrícola
third town	9. **tértium óppidum**	9. a sixth son	sextus fílius
ninth queen	10. **nona regina**	10. four friends	quáttuor amici

51

VOCABULARY

Say each number aloud and have students repeat after you.

Do not say the gender endings for **unus** or the ordinal numbers when reciting the numbers. The goal here is for students to say these numbers in order just as we do in English. Students need much practice with cardinal and ordinal numbers. Especially troublesome is **novem** (9), **nonus** (9th), and **novus** (*new*).

Pronunciation helps:
u as in *food*
c and **g** are soft before **e, i, ae, oe**
soft **c** = /ch/

Derivatives:
     union, unity
     duet, duel, dual
     triune, triangle, trinity
     September
     October, octopus, octogon
     November, novena
     December, decimate
     primal, primary
     secondary
     tertiary
     quart, quarter
     quintuplets
     sextuplets

GRAMMAR - CHALK TALK

What verb never takes a direct object? (the *to be* verb, **sum**) What follows a linking verb? (a noun or an adjective in the predicate) **Diagram: Puella est bona**. Draw an arrow from the predicate adjective to the subject.

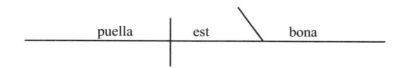

Predicate nominatives and adjectives seem to be difficult concepts for students. The predicate is the part of the sentence that contains the verb (see pages 94-100 of text appendix). A predicate nominative is in the predicate part of the sentence and renames the subject. A predicate adjective is in the predicate part of the sentence and describes the subject. Predicate nominatives and adjectives follow *linking verbs*. They are in the nominative case. The only linking verb used in this book is the verb **sum**. All other verbs are action verbs.

LESSON XX

1 **ORAL RECITATION/REVIEW**
Greeting
Teacher: *Recitemus*

>**personal & tense endings**
>**1st conj. p.p. endings**
>**amo** - six tenses, p.p.
>**do, sto, juvo, lavo,** p.p.
>**sum** - six tenses, p.p.
>**case names**
>**mensa, ae**
>**servus, i**
>**bellum, i**
>**bonus, bona, bonum**
>**unus, duo ...**
>**primus, secundus ...**

Grammar Review Questions: 1-92

LESSON XX
UNIT III REVIEW

First and Second Declension Nouns

Case	1st Declension S.	1st Declension Pl.	2nd Declension Masculine S.	2nd Declension Masculine Pl.	2nd Declension Neuter S.	2nd Declension Neuter Pl.
nom.	mensa	mensae	servus	servi	bellum	bella
gen.	mensae	mensarum	servi	servorum	belli	bellorum
dat.	mensae	mensis	servo	servis	bello	bellis
acc.	mensam	mensas	servum	servos	bellum	bella
abl.	mensā	mensis	servo	servis	bello	bellis

First and Second Declension Adjectives

Case	Singular M.	Singular F.	Singular N.	Plural M.	Plural F.	Plural N.
nom.	bonus	bona	bonum	boni	bonae	bona
gen.	boni	bonae	boni	bonorum	bonarum	bonorum
dat.	bono	bonae	bono	bonis	bonis	bonis
acc.	bonum	bonam	bonum	bonos	bonas	bona
abl.	bono	bonā	bono	bonis	bonis	bonis

Numbers

Roman Numerals	Cardinal		Ordinal	
I	unus -a -um	one	primus -a -um	first
II	duo	two	secundus -a -um	second
III	tres	three	tértius -a -um	third
IV	quáttuor	four	quartus -a -um	fourth
V	quinque	five	quintus -a -um	fifth
VI	sex	six	sextus -a -um	sixth
VII	septem	seven	séptimus -a -um	seventh
VIII	octo	eight	octavus -a -um	eighth
IX	novem	nine	nonus -a -um	ninth
X	decem	ten	décimus -a -um	tenth

52

This lesson is for the purpose of review, consolidation, and mastery of vocabulary and declensions.
Make copies of workbook pages to use as drill sheets and practice tests.

MASTERY GOALS FOR GRAMMAR AND VOCABULARY
1) Be able to recite and write the declension of the three model nouns, **mensa**, **servus**, and **bellum**.
2) Be able to recite and write the declension all thirty nouns correctly.
3) Be able to pronounce and spell all adjectives and all thirty nouns, Latin to English and English to Latin.
   Be able to give the genitive singular, gender, and declension of each noun.
4) Know and be able to apply the four gender rules.
5) Be able to recite and write the five cases in order. Be able to give the job of each case.
6) Know Latin Sayings, Latin to English and English to Latin.
7) Recite **bonus**, **bona**, **bonum** in adjective form.
8) Recite cardinal and ordinal numbers in order.

See Teacher Guidelines for Games and Review Activities.

There is a test for this unit.

Vocabulary Review

aeternus -a -um	*eternal, everlasting*	**equus -i m.**	*horse*	**parvus -a -um**	*small*
agnus -i m.	*lamb*	**fílius -i m.**	*son*	**poeta -ae m.**	*poet*
agrícola -ae m.	*farmer*	**forum -i n.**	*forum, marketplace*	**puella -ae f.**	*girl*
altus -a -um	*high, deep*	**Itália -ae f.**	*Italy*	**regina -ae f.**	*queen*
amicus -i m.	*friend*	**latus -a -um**	*wide, broad*	**regnum -i n.**	*kingdom*
annus -i m.	*year*	**magnus -a -um**	*great, large*	**Roma -ae f.**	*Rome*
bellum -i n.	*war*	**malus -a -um**	*bad*	**sanctus -a -um**	*sacred, holy*
bonus -a -um	*good*	**Maria -ae f.**	*Mary*	**saxum -i n.**	*rock*
caelum -i n.	*sky, heaven*	**mensa -ae f.**	*table*	**servus -i m.**	*slave, servant*
Christus -i m.	*Christ*	**multus -a -um**	*much, many*	**templum -i n.**	*temple*
débitum -i n.	*debt, sin*	**mundus -i m.**	*world, mankind*	**terra -ae f.**	*earth, land*
deus -i m.	*god*	**nauta -ae m.**	*sailor*	**verbum -i n.**	*word*
dóminus -i m.	*lord, master*	**novus -a -um**	*new*		
donum -i n.	*gift*	**óppidum -i n.**	*town*		

Grammar Review

♦ Four gender rules: (1) **NG** (2) **1D F** (3) **2D us M** (4) **2D um N**

♦ The neuter rule. For every neuter noun the nominative and accusative case forms are identical, and the nominative and accusative plural ending is **-a**.

♦ A verb agrees with its subject in person and number.

♦ An adjective agrees with its noun in gender, number, and case, and may precede or follow its noun.

♦ A noun or adjective in the predicate that follows a linking verb and renames or describes the subject is in the nominative case and is called a predicate nominative or a predicate adjective.

♦ The genitive singular of a 1st declension noun is **-ae**, and of a 2nd declension noun is **-i**.

Latin Sayings

Roma Aeterna   Anno Dómini (A.D.)   ante bellum
Quáttuor anni témpora   Mater Italiae Roma

MINI-MILESTONE

This is a mini-milestone for your students. They have learned three model nouns and two of the five declensions. They are only three declensions left and four model nouns before reaching the next Milestone Marker. You will be there in no time!

UNIT IV INTRODUCTION

The purpose of the Unit Introductions is to give you and your students an overview of the content of the unit. You are not expected to understand all of the concepts, but it is helpful to have a quick introduction of terms and ideas that the students will be encountering.

The Unit Introduction also helps students to see the big picture, to see each lesson as part of a whole that all fits together. Learning is a journey. To look back at where you have been and look forward to where you are going motivates the student and gives encouragement for the work ahead.

UNIT IV INTRODUCTION

♦ There are five declensions in Latin. Declensions 1 and 2 are similar and were studied in Unit III.

♦ Declensions 3-5 will be studied in this unit.

♦ The 3rd declension is the largest declension. 3rd declension nouns are more challenging than 1st and 2nd declension nouns.

♦ 3rd declension nouns may change spelling significantly from the nominative to the genitive. The genitive form must be written out in full.

lex legis   **flumen flúminis**

♦ The 3rd declension has all three genders, but masculine and feminine nouns have identical case endings. Thus, there are only two models to learn in the 3rd declension.[8]

1) masculine/feminine   2) neuter

♦ There are no gender-specific nominative endings in the 3rd declension. The gender of each noun must be memorized individually.

♦ There are 3rd declension adjectives but they will not be studied in this text.

♦ The 4th and 5th declensions have few nouns and no adjectives. Most 4th declension nouns are masculine; most 5th declension nouns are feminine.

54

UNIT IV
NOUNS
3RD, 4TH, AND 5TH DECLENSIONS

Colosseum today (top), model (below)

55

55

LESSON XXI

① ORAL RECITATION/REVIEW
Greeting
Teacher: *Recitemus*

      personal & tense endings
      1st conj. p.p. endings
      amo - six tenses, p.p.
      do, sto, juvo, lavo - p.p.
      sum - six tenses, p.p.
      case names
      mensa, ae
      servus, i
      bellum, i
      bonus, bona, bonum
      unus, duo ...
      primus, secundus ...

Grammar Review Questions: 1-92

② LATIN SAYING

Say aloud and ask students to repeat after you.

almus -a -um *adj.*   nurturing
mater matris *f.*   mother

This saying illustrates the rather difficult concept of a 1st-2nd declension adjective modifying a 3rd declension noun. They agree in gender, number, and case, but not declension.

LESSON XXI

	alma mater	*nurturing mother*

Third Declension   Masculine and Feminine

stem **patr-**

Case	Singular	Ending	Plural	Ending
nom.	pater	-	patr**es**	-es
gen.	patr**is**	-is	patr**um**	-um
dat.	patr**i**	-i	pátr**ibus**	-ibus
acc.	patr**em**	-em	patr**es**	-es
abl.	patr**e**	-e	pátr**ibus**	-ibus

♦ Masculine and feminine nouns of the *3rd Declension* have the same case endings.

♦ There is no characteristic nominative singular ending in the 3rd declension. The chart has a dash to show that the nominative singular form is variable.

♦ The change in spelling from the nominative to the genitive form can be significant. In a dictionary entry the genitive form must be written out in full as shown below.

♦ The nominative singular cannot be used to find the stem. To find the stem of a 3rd declension noun, drop the genitive singular ending, **is**.

Vocabulary

dux ducis	*m.*	leader	*duke*
frater fratris	*m.*	brother	*fraternity*
mater matris	*f.*	mother	*maternity*
miles mílitis	*m.*	soldier	*military*
pater patris	*m.*	father	*patrician*
rex regis	*m.*	king	*regal*
soror sororis	*f.*	sister	*sorority*

56

---

④ GRAMMAR - CHALK TALK
3rd Declension stem and declension. Write the declension of pater and the case endings on the board. Latin is a language of stems and endings. Look at the grammar chart carefully. What is the stem for the declension of pater? (**patr**) Which form gives you the stem, the nominative or the genitive? (genitive) How do you find the stem of a 3rd declension noun? (Drop the case ending **-is** from the genitive singular.) Why is there a blank in the nominative singular of the grammar chart? (There is no characteristic ending for the 3rd declension.) Say the 3rd declension aloud for students, using the word *blank* for the nominative singular ending. Have students repeat *in choro* several times. Write the 1st and 2nd declension case endings next to the 3rd declension and compare and contrast.

Memorize the declension of *pater* and the 3rd declension M/F case endings.

Use the *Disappearing Line Technique* as described in the Teaching Guidelines.

Word Study • Grammar • Syntax

◆ Because the nominative singular ending is variable and doesn't necessarily provide the stem, the generalization for Latin nouns of all declensions is:

> Memorize the genitive singular of every Latin noun carefully. The genitive singular (1) identifies the declension of the noun and (2) provides the stem.

◆ The 3rd declension has all three genders. The nouns in this list all have natural gender.

◆ 3rd declension nouns can be modified by 1st/2nd declension adjectives. The adjective agrees with its noun in gender, number, and case, but not declension.

| good father | **pater bonus** | good fathers | **patres boni** |
| good mother | **mater bona** | good mothers | **matres bonae** |

Alma mater refers to the school one graduates from. John Cardinal Newman said a university should be an alma mater, "knowing her children one by one, not a foundry, or a mint or a treadmill."

Oral Drill - Nominative Case

soldiers	1.	**mílites**	1.	leaders	duces
sisters	2.	**sorores**	2.	king	rex
king	3.	**rex**	3.	sisters	sorores
brothers	4.	**fratres**	4.	soldier	miles
leader	5.	**dux**	5.	soldiers	mílites
mother	6.	**mater**	6.	brother	frater
sons	7.	**fílii**	7.	kings	reges
sister	8.	**soror**	8.	father	pater
wars	9.	**bella**	9.	girls	puellae
fathers	10.	**patres**	10.	leader	dux

57

VOCABULARY ③

Say each noun aloud with its genitive form and meaning. Have students repeat after you.

1) 3rd declension words are much more challenging than 1st-2nd decl. words. Practice saying both nominative and genitive forms until students are comfortable with them.
2) Why are **mater** and **soror** feminine? (natural gender - They name female persons.) Why are the other five nouns masculine? (natural gender - They name male persons. In the Roman world only men were leaders or soldiers.)
3) Do all of these words end in the same letters in the nominative (**a, us, um**) like the other declensions you have learned? (No!)
4) Why is the genitive form written out in full? (because the spelling changes)

Pronunciation helps:
g and **c** are soft before **e, i** and **ae**; hard before **a, o, u**.

Derivatives:
   paternal, paternity, patriarch
   maternal, matrimony
   Tyrannosaurus Rex
   aqueduct
   militia

GRAMMAR - CHALK TALK
Look at **Bullet 5**, and give two reasons why the genitive singular form of every noun is important.

Adjective agreement. Look at the adjectives in Lesson 18. What endings do they have? (1st/2nd declension M/F/N endings) These adjectives are called 1st/2nd declension adjectives. What happens if you want to use one of these adjectives with a 3rd declension noun? Can they agree? (yes) What is the rule for agreement between a noun and its adjective? (An adjective agrees with its noun in gender, number, and case.) A noun and its adjective do not have to agree in declension. Write examples from **Bullet 7** on the board and give some examples for classroom practice.

LESSON XXII

1 **ORAL RECITATION/REVIEW**
Greeting
Teacher: *Recitemus*

  personal & tense endings
  1st conj. p.p. endings
  amo - six tenses, p.p.
  do, sto, juvo, lavo - p.p.
  sum - six tenses, p.p.
  case names
  mensa, ae
  servus, i
  bellum, i
  bonus -a -um
  unus, duo ...
  primus, secundus ...
  pater, patris

Grammar Review Questions: 1-96

2 **LATIN SAYING**
Say aloud and ask students to repeat after you.

pax pacis *f.*	peace
Romanus -a -um *adj.*	Roman

This saying, like the one in the previous lesson, illustrates the concept of a 1st-2nd declension adjective modifying a 3rd declension noun. They agree in gender, number, and case, but not declension. (**Romanus** can be a noun or an adjective.)

LESSON XXII

Pax Romana   *The Roman Peace*

Third Declension   Masculine and Feminine

stem **leg-**

Case	Singular	Ending	Plural	Ending
nom.	lex	-	leg es	-es
gen.	leg is	-is	leg um	-um
dat.	leg i	-i	lég ibus	-ibus
acc.	leg em	-em	leg es	-es
abl.	leg e	-e	lég ibus	-ibus

♦ The 3rd declension nouns in the previous lesson had natural gender. The nouns in this lesson have grammatical gender. The case endings are the same.

♦ The grammatical gender of 3rd declension nouns must be memorized individually. There are no characteristic endings such as **a, us,** or **um** to indicate the gender of a 3rd declension noun.

Vocabulary

canis canis	*m. or f.*	dog	*canine*
crux crucis	*f.*	cross	*crucify*
lex legis	*f.*	law	*legal*
lux lucis	*f.*	light	*lucid, Lucifer*
mos moris	*m.*	custom	*moral*
panis panis	*m.*	bread	*companion*
pax pacis	*f.*	peace	*pacific*
pes pedis	*m.*	foot	*pedal*
sol solis	*m.*	sun	*solar*
vox vocis	*f.*	voice	*vocal*

*Oral Drill for Lesson XXII is on page 113.

58

---

4 **GRAMMAR - CHALK TALK**
Look at the grammar chart closely. Is the declension of **lex** different from **pater**? (No) The vocabulary words in Lesson 21 had what kind of gender? (natural gender) The vocabulary words in this lesson have what kind of gender? (grammatical except **canis**, which technically has *common* gender* because it can be masculine or feminine)

Third declension nouns do not have gender specific endings like the 1st/2nd declension (**a, us, um**), so you will have to work harder to learn the gender of 3rd declension nouns. Although there are no gender specific endings in the nominative, there are some generalizations that help. One of those is that most 3rd declension nouns that end in **x** are feminine. But why is **rex** masculine? (it has natural gender) Natural gender trumps all other gender rules.

For this text the gender of these 3rd declension nouns is easy to remember. The nouns that end in **x** in the nominative singular are feminine, and the rest are masculine.

There is not a new grammar paradigm to learn in this lesson, just more practice with 3rd declension nouns. Students should be able to decline **lex**, or any 3rd declension noun, but it will not be added to the recitation.

*This can be indicated by *m./f.* or by *c.* in a dictionary.

Word Study • Grammar • Syntax

◆ As you learn more 3rd declension nouns you will begin to see patterns that will help you remember the gender of each noun. For instance, 3rd declension nouns that end in **x** are usually feminine. Remember, however, that natural gender *trumps* grammatical gender. Even though most nouns that end in **x** are feminine, **rex** and **dux** are masculine because of natural gender.

◆ English words that show their 3rd declension origin by retaining the Latin plural ending **-es** are:

synopsis, synopses	*crisis, crises*	*index, indices*
appendix, appendices	*matrix, matrices*	*axis, axes*

The **Pax Romana** was the era of peace and prosperity that began with the principate of Caesar Augustus and continued for the next two hundred years. The British Empire was sometimes referred to as the *Pax Britannia* and the present world order is often called the *Pax Americana*.

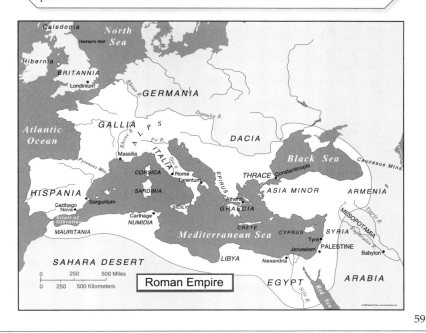

Roman Empire

59

VOCABULARY

③

Say each noun aloud with its genitive form and meaning. Have students repeat after you.

Look at all of the words in the vocabulary list. Do any name living things? (Only **canis**) Do any of them have natural gender? (Only **canis**, which can be either gender) What kind of gender do the other words have? (grammatical gender) How can you determine the gender of a 3rd declension noun that doesn't have natural gender? (You have to learn the gender of each individual word.) Can you see a plan to help you remember the gender of these 10 words? (The five that end in the letter **x** are feminine, **canis** has natural gender, and the other four words are masculine.)

Pronunciation helps:
g and **c** are soft before **e**, **i** and **ae**; hard before **a**, **o**, **u**.

Derivatives:
>   *legislature*
>   *pacify, pacifier*
>   *crucifixion, crucial*
>   *pantry*
>   *centipede, pedestrian*
>   *impede, impediment*
>   *solstice, parasol*
>   *morality*

GRAMMAR - CHALK TALK

The purpose of this lesson is to give students an additional week to learn the 3rd declension and to help students with the gender of 3rd declension nouns. This declension is identical to the one in the previous lesson.

This is a good time to check your pronunciation skills with reference to hard and soft **c** and **g** as you decline **lex**, **vox**, etc.

Use this week to study the grammar appendix on pages 93-106 in the Student Text. Solidify sentence labeling, diagramming skills, and the four sentence patterns covered in this text.

NOTE ON PANIS: Panis ends in **-ium** instead of **-um** in the genitive plural. This type of noun is called an **i-stem** and will be fully explained in *Second Form*. **Panis** is included in *First Form* because of its presence in the **Pater Noster**. For now, do not have students decline it in the genitive plural.

LESSON XXIII

1 **ORAL RECITATION/REVIEW**
Greeting
Teacher: *Recitemus*

    personal & tense endings
    1st conj. p.p. endings
    amo - six tenses, p.p.
    do, sto, juvo, lavo - p.p.
    sum - six tenses
    case names
    mensa, ae
    servus, i
    bellum, i
    pater, patris
    bonus -a -um
    unus, duo ...
    primus, secundus ...

Grammar Review Questions: 1-99

2 **LATIN SAYING**
Say aloud and ask students to repeat after you..

caput cápitis *n.*	head
mundus -i *m.*	world
mundi *gen. sing.*	

Caput Mundi   *Head of the World*

Third Declension   Neuter
stem: **nómin-**

Case	Singular	Ending	Plural	Ending
nom.	nomen	-	nómin a	-a
gen.	nómin is	-is	nómin um	-um
dat.	nómin i	-i	nómin ibus	-ibus
acc.	nomen	-	nómin a	-a
abl.	nómin e	-e	nómin ibus	-ibus

♦ **Nomen** is the model noun chosen to illustrate 3rd declension neuter nouns.

♦ There is no characteristic nominative singular ending for 3rd declension neuter nouns. The chart has a dash to show that the nominative singular form is variable.

♦ All nouns whose genitive singular ends in **is** belong to the 3rd declension.

♦ To find the stem, drop the genitive singular ending, **is**.

Vocabulary

caput cápitis	*n.*	head	*capital*
cor cordis	*n.*	heart	*cordial*
flumen flúminis	*n.*	river	*fluid*
lumen lúminis	*n.*	lamp	*luminous*
nomen nóminis	*n.*	name	*nominate*

60

---

4 **GRAMMAR - CHALK TALK**
The 3rd declension has two subgroups. Can you name them? (1. masculine/feminine nouns 2. neuter nouns)
The 3rd declension has all three genders just like the 1st/2nd declension group.

Stem. What is the rule for finding the stem of a Latin noun? (Drop the case ending from the genitive singular)
Write **nomen nóminis** on the board. What is the stem? (**nomin**) Compare the nominative form with the stem.
(**nomen - nomin**)

Declension of *nomen*. Recreate the declension of **nomen** on the board in steps. First write nomen and then complete your two columns with the stem **nomin**. Ask students for the case endings. Add them to your chart, pointing out that in the accusative singular, the stem reverts back to the nominative form, nomen.

What is the neuter rule? **Bullet 5.**
Write the case endings for the 2nd declension neuter on the board to show how they also obey the neuter rule.

Word Study • Grammar • Syntax

◆ There are neuter nouns in the 2nd, 3rd, and 4th declensions. All neuter nouns obey the neuter rule:

the nominative and accusative case forms are identical
the nominative and accusative plural case ending is -a

◆ English words that show their 3rd declension neuter origin by retaining the Latin plural ending **-a** are:

corpus, corpora   *genus, genera*   *viscus, viscera*

> **Caput Mundi.** According to legend, workmen discovered a perfectly preserved human head while digging for the foundation of the Temple of Jupiter on the Saturnian Hill. When asked the meaning of this strange omen, the augurs responded that it meant Rome would become the head city of the world. The Saturnian Hill was renamed the Capitoline Hill from which we derive our word *Capitol.*

Oral Drill - Nominative Case

heads	1. **cápita**		1. heart	cor	
river	2. **flumen**		2. lamps	lúmina	
hearts	3. **corda**		3. rivers	flúmina	
foot	4. **pes**		4. names	nómina	
lamps	5. **lúmina**		5. feet	pedes	
heart	6. **cor**		6. lamp	lumen	
leaders	7. **duces**		7. river	flumen	
lamp	8. **lumen**		8. heads	cápita	
rivers	9. **flúmina**		9. leader	dux	
head	10. **caput**		10. head	caput	

61

VOCABULARY ③

Say each noun aloud with its genitive form and meaning. Have students repeat after you.

This is a short vocabulary list because these are difficult words. Pay careful attention to the change in spelling from the nominative to the genitive. Why is the genitive singular form written out in full? (because the spelling changes) What is the genitive singular ending? **(is)** What does that tell you? (**Bullet 3**, the words belong to the 3rd declension) Three words rhyme. What are they? **(nomen, flumen, lumen)**

Derivatives:
*   nomination, noun*
*   nominative*
*   flume, fluent*
*   illuminate*
*   capitalize, Capitol*
*   core, courage*

Now is a good time to teach the difference between capital and Capitol.

Memorize the declension of *nomen* and the 3rd declension neuter case endings.

LESSON XXIV

❶ ORAL RECITATION/REVIEW
Greeting

Teacher: *Recitemus*

personal & tense endings
1st conj. p.p. endings
amo - six tenses, p.p.
do, sto, juvo, lavo - p.p.
sum - six tenses, p.p.
case names
mensa, ae
servus, i
bellum, i
pater, patris
nomen, nóminis
bonus -a -um
unus, duo ...
primus, secundus ...

Grammar Review Questions: 1-99

❷ LATIN SAYING
Say aloud and ask students to repeat after you.

rex regis *m.*   king
  rex *nom. sing.*
  regum *gen. pl.*

Rex Regum   *King of Kings*

Third Declension Review

Case	Masculine/Feminine S.	Pl.	Neuter S.	Pl.
nom.	pater	patr**es**	nomen	nómin**a**
gen.	patr**is**	patr**um**	nómin**is**	nómin**um**
dat.	patr**i**	pátr**ibus**	nómin**i**	nómin**ibus**
acc.	patr**em**	patr**es**	nomen	nómin**a**
abl.	patr**e**	pátr**ibus**	nómin**e**	nómin**ibus**

♦ Contrast and compare the masculine, feminine, and neuter nouns of the 3rd declension. How are they alike and how are they different?

♦ All nouns whose genitive singular ends in **is** belong to the 3rd declension.

♦ To find the stem, drop the genitive singular ending, **is**.

Vocabulary Review

canis canis *m.* or *f.*	dog		**miles mílitis** *m.*	soldier
caput cápitis *n.*	head		**mos moris** *m.*	custom
cor cordis *n.*	heart		**nomen nóminis** *n.*	name
crux crucis *f.*	cross		**panis panis** *m.*	bread
dux ducis *m.*	leader		**pater patris** *m.*	father
flumen flúminis *n.*	river		**pax pacis** *f.*	peace
frater fratris *m.*	brother		**pes pedis** *m.*	foot
lex legis *f.*	law		**rex regis** *m.*	king
lumen lúminis *n.*	lamp		**sol solis** *m.*	sun
lux lucis *f.*	light		**soror sororis** *f.*	sister
mater matris *f.*	mother		**vox vocis** *f.*	voice

62

---

❹ GRAMMAR - CHALK TALK

The 3rd declension has all three genders, but unlike the 1st and 2nd declensions, the masculine and feminine nouns do not have different case endings. In addition, there are no characteristic nominative endings to signal the gender of a noun. Students must memorize the gender of each noun individually. However, there are many generalizations that are an aid to remembering the gender of these nouns. In *Second Form*, we will start a list of gender rules for the 3rd declension.

(The 3rd declension also has i-stem nouns, but they are not covered in this text, so students only have two paradigms to learn for this declension, which is manageable. **Canis** looks like an i-stem but is not.)

What is the normal word order of an English sentence? (subject - verb - direct object)
What is the normal word order of a Latin sentence? (subject - direct object - verb)
What is the direct object case? (accusative)

Write on the board: **Mary praises the queen.**   **The queen praises Mary.**

Ask students to label these sentences.   SN   V-t   A   DO

Word Study • Grammar • Syntax

◆ The direct object of a verb is in the accusative case.

Regina laudat.	The queen praises. (no direct object)
<u>Reginam</u> laudat.	He (she) praises the queen. (queen is the direct object)

In the second sentence the subject must be in the verb because **reginam,** in the accusative case, cannot be a subject. See *Sentence Pattern #2* on page 97.

◆ Word order determines the subject and direct object in English, but not in Latin, where words can be in any order and still mean the same thing. The three sentences below all mean *Mary praises the queen.*

DO SN V-t	V-t DO SN	SN DO V-t
Reginam Maria laudat.	**Laudat reginam Maria.**	**Maria reginam laudat.**

◆ A common word order in Latin is: **subject   direct object   verb.**

> **Rex Regum.** Christ is known as the *King of Kings.*

Oral Drill - Nominative case

soldiers	1. **mílites**	1.	fathers	patres
heads	2. **cápita**	2.	heads	cápita
names	3. **nómina**	3.	kings	reges
leaders	4. **duces**	4.	lamp	lumen
rivers	5. **flúmina**	5.	soldier	miles
kings	6. **reges**	6.	soldiers	mílites
fathers	7. **patres**	7.	names	nómina
sister	8. **soror**	8.	customs	mores
laws	9. **leges**	9.	voices	voces
dog	10. **canis**	10.	sisters	sorores

63

VOCABULARY　　③

Say each noun aloud with its genitive form and meaning. Have students repeat after you.

Third declension nouns are very challenging. This lesson allows for a thorough review and mastery learning.

The major difficulty in the 3rd declension at this point is to remember the five neuter nouns and to decline them with neuter endings.

GRAMMAR - CHALK TALK

Does word order indicate the subject and direct object in English? (Yes) Is word order important in English? (Yes)

Write on the board. **Maria reginam laudat.**　　**Reginam Maria laudat.**　　**Laudat reginam Maria.**
Ask students to label and translate each sentence.

Does word order indicate the subject and direct object in Latin? (No, the case ending shows the subject and direct object.) Is word order important in Latin? (not as much as English) Are there times when you can't tell the direct object by the case ending? (Yes, neuter nouns and 3rd declension plural nouns.)

LESSON XXV

① ORAL RECITATION/REVIEW
Greeting
Teacher: *Recitemus*

> **personal & tense endings**
> **1st conj. p.p. endings**
> **amo** - six tenses, p.p.
> **do, sto, juvo, lavo** - p.p.
> **sum** - six tenses, p.p.
> **case names**
> **mensa, ae**
> **servus, i**
> **bellum, i**
> **pater, patris**
> **nomen, nóminis**
> **bonus -a -um**
> **unus, duo ...**
> **primus, secundus ...**

Grammar Review Questions: 1-103

② LATIN SAYING
Say aloud and ask students to repeat after you.

Senatus -ūs *m.*	The Senate
populus -i *m.*	people
Romanus -a -um *adj.*	Roman
-que	and

Que is an enclitic (a word attached to another word). **Que** is used to attach two closely related things, like *boys* **and** *girls*, or *bread* **and** *butter*. The accent is always on the syllable directly preceding the **-que**, and will be indicated by an accent mark. The literal translation is *The Roman Senate and People,* which does not sound quite as majestic as the one given.

Senatus Populúsque Romanus (S.P.Q.R.)
The Senate and People of Rome

Fourth Declension
stem **port-**

Case	Singular	Ending	Plural	Ending
nom.	port**us**	-us	port**ūs**	-ūs
gen.	port**ūs**	-ūs	pórt**uum**	-uum
dat.	pórt**ui**	-ui	pórt**ibus**	-ibus
acc.	port**um**	-um	port**ūs**	-ūs
abl.	port**u**	-u	pórt**ibus**	-ibus

♦ **Portus** is the model noun chosen to illustrate the *4th Declension.*

♦ All nouns whose genitive singular end in **-ūs** belong to the 4th declension.

♦ To find the stem, drop the genitive singular ending, **-ūs**.

♦ The genitive singular, nominative and accusative plural will be marked with macrons in this text to distinguish them from the nominative singular ending.

Vocabulary

adventus -ūs	*m.*	arrival	*advent*
domus -ūs	*f.*	house, home	*domestic*
exércitus -ūs	*m.*	army	*exercise*
fructus -ūs	*m.*	fruit	*fruit*
lacus -ūs	*m.*	lake	
manus -ūs	*f.*	hand	*manual, manufacture*
metus -ūs	*m.*	fear	
portus -ūs	*m.*	harbor	*port*
senatus -ūs	*m.*	senate	*senate*
spíritus -ūs	*m.*	spirit	*spirit*

64

④ GRAMMAR - CHALK TALK
We are on the home stretch. Only two small declensions to go. Even though these declensions have relatively few words, the paradigm has to be memorized nonetheless. What is the stem of **portus**? (port) How do you find the stem of a Latin noun? (drop the case ending from the genitive singular) Write **port** on the board ten times and ask a student for the singular endings and write on the board and then do the same with the plural. Compare and contrast to the 3rd declension M/F endings. The macron is used on the genitive singular and nominative and accusative plural forms to distinguish them from the nominative singular.

> ****Memorize the declension of *portus* and the 4th declension case endings.****

Use the *Disappearing Line Technique* as described in the Teaching Guidelines.

Word Study • Grammar • Syntax

♦ The gender rule for the 4th declension is **4D M**. Most 4th declension nouns are masculine. A few are feminine but both genders have the same endings. There are a few neuter nouns that have slightly different case endings. The 4th declension is a small declension with relatively few nouns.

♦ The 2nd, 3rd, and 4th declensions have nouns that end in -**us** in the nominative singular: You have had -**us** nouns in the 2nd and 4th declensions.

2nd declension	servus, servi
4th declension	portus, portūs

Senatus Populúsque Romanus. S.P.Q.R. is the symbol of the Roman Republic written on all official government documents and monuments. It is similar to the *Office of the President* in America or *O.H.M.S., On Her Majesty's Service,* in England.

Oral Drill - Nominative Case

harbor	1. **portus**		1. hand	manus
hands	2. **manūs**		2. years	anni
year	3. **annus**		3. houses	domūs
fruit	4. **fructus**		4. arrival	adventus
spirit	5. **spíritus**		5. harbors	portūs
senate	6. **senatus**		6. fruit	fructus
slave	7. **servus**		7. lakes	lacūs
lakes	8. **lacūs**		8. spirits	spíritūs
Christ	9. **Christus**		9. fear	metus
army	10. **exércitus**		10. slaves	servi

65

VOCABULARY

Say each noun aloud with its genitive form and meaning. Have students repeat after you.

What two letters do these nouns end in? (**us**) What is the genitive singular ending? (**ūs**) What gender are most of these nouns? (masculine) Compare these nouns to the 2nd declension masculine nouns. (The 2nd declension masculine nouns also end in **us** in the nominative, but the genitive singular is **i** and the case endings are different.)

Pronunciation helps:
soft **c** is /**ch**/
g and **c** are soft before **e, i** and **ae**; hard before **a, o, u.**

Derivatives:
   adventure
   domicile
   seaport, airport
   senator
   spiritual

LESSON XXVI

① ORAL RECITATION/REVIEW
Greeting
Teacher: *Recitemus*

    personal & tense endings
    1st conj. p.p. endings
    amo - six tenses, p.p.
    do, sto, juvo, lavo - p.p.
    sum - six tenses, p.p.
    case names
    mensa, ae
    servus, i
    bellum, i
    pater, patris
    nomen, nóminis
    portus, ūs
    bonus -a -um
    unus, duo ...
    primus, secundus ...

Grammar Review Questions: 1-105

② LATIN SAYING
Say aloud and ask students to repeat after you.

dies diei *m.*	day
diem *acc. case*	
carpo *(3rd conj.)*	to take, seize

Carpe is the imperative mood (for commands) like **ora** and **labora** in Lesson 11. The principal parts for **carpo** are **carpo, cárpere, carpsi, carptus.**

LESSON XXVI

Carpe diem.   *Seize the day.*

Fifth Declension
stem   **r-**

Case	Singular	Ending	Plural	Ending
nom.	res	-es	res	-es
gen.	rei	-ei	rerum	-erum
dat.	rei	-ei	rebus	-ebus
acc.	rem	-em	res	-es
abl.	re	-e	rebus	-ebus

♦ **Res** is the model noun chosen to illustrate the *5th Declension.*

♦ All nouns whose genitive singular end in **ei** belong to the 5th declension.

♦ To find the stem drop the genitive singular ending, **ei.**

Vocabulary

dies diei	*m.*	day		*diary*
fácies faciei	*f.*	face		*facial*
fides fídei	*f*	faith, trust		*fidelity*
res rei	*f.*	thing, matter, affair, business		*real*
spes spei	*f.*	hope		*despair*

66

---

④ GRAMMAR - CHALK TALK
What is the stem of res? (**r**) Write the stem ten times on the board and then add the case endings. Compare and contrast to the 3rd declension endings. How do you say *thing* as a subject? (**res**) *things* as a subject? (**res**) Can you think of any English words that have the same spelling in the singular and plural? (sheep, scissors, deer, moose, fish)

        Memorize the declension of *res* and the 5th declension case endings.

Use the *Disappearing Line Technique* as described in the Teaching Guidelines.

Class practice: Write the nominative form of each vocabulary word on the board and find the stem by dropping the **es**. Although the general rule for finding the stem of any Latin noun is to drop the genitive singular ending, there are so many consecutive vowels in these words that students can easily become confused. In the 5th declension it is safer to always think of dropping the **es** from the nominative form and then adding the endings. To write the genitive form think - substitute **ei** for **es.**

Word Study • Grammar • Syntax

- The gender rule for the 5th declension is **5D F.** Most 5th declension nouns are feminine. The 5th declension is small and has few nouns. A few are masculine, and none are neuter.

- Because the stem of a 5th declension noun can end in the letter **i**, a genitive singular form can have three consecutive vowels all of which are pronounced - **faciei**.

Carpe diem. From one of Horace's *Odes,* **carpe diem** can be interpreted to mean, "make the most of today; take hold of the day and use it well, for tomorrow is not promised to you." Today is all you have.

Oral Drill - Nominative Case

face, faces	**1.**	**fácies**	1.	days	dies
day, days	**2.**	**dies**	2.	things	res
faith, faiths	**3.**	**fides**	3.	face	fácies
soldier	**4.**	**miles**	4.	faces	fácies
soldiers	**5.**	**mílites**	5.	arrival	adventus
kings	**6.**	**reges**	6.	trust	fides
thing, things	**7.**	**res**	7.	thing	res
rivers	**8.**	**flúmina**	8.	hope	spes
hearts	**9.**	**corda**	9.	faith	fides
hope, hopes	**10.**	**spes**	10.	home	domus

67

VOCABULARY ③

Say each noun aloud with its genitive form and meaning. Have students repeat after you.

5th-declension nouns other than **dies** and **res** do not always have a full plural declension. For example, **fácies** only occurs in the plural in the nominative/ accusative. Students at this level, however, do not need to worry about this level of detail.

Pronunciation helps:
C is hard before **a, o, u,** and soft /**ch**/ before **e, i, ae.** **S** is always pronounced **s**, never **z**. Two of these words have genitive forms with three vowels, all of which are pronounced.

Derivatives:
dial
facade
infidel
desperate

LESSON XXVII

1 **ORAL RECITATION/REVIEW**
Greeting
Teacher: *Recitemus*

       personal & tense endings
       1st conj. p.p. endings
       amo - six tenses, p.p.
       do, sto, juvo, lavo - p.p.
       sum - six tenses, p.p.
       case names
       mensa, ae
       servus, i
       bellum, i
       pater, patris
       nomen, nóminis
       portus, ūs
       res, rei
       bonus -a -um
       unus, duo ...
       primus, secundus ...

Grammar Review Questions: 1-107

LESSON XXVII

UNIT IV REVIEW

Third, Fourth, Fifth Declensions

Case	3rd Declension M/F S.	3rd Declension M/F Pl.	3rd Declension Neuter S.	3rd Declension Neuter Pl.
nom.	pat**er**	patr**es**	nomen	nómin**a**
gen.	patr**is**	patr**um**	nómin**is**	nómin**um**
dat.	patr**i**	patr**ibus**	nómin**i**	nomín**ibus**
acc.	patr**em**	patr**es**	nomen	nómin**a**
abl.	patr**e**	patr**ibus**	nómin**e**	nomín**ibus**

Case	4th Declension S.	4th Declension Pl.	5th Declension S.	5th Declension Pl.
nom.	port**us**	port**ūs**	r**es**	r**es**
gen.	port**ūs**	pórt**uum**	r**ei**	r**erum**
dat.	pórt**ui**	pórt**ibus**	r**ei**	r**ebus**
acc.	port**um**	port**ūs**	r**em**	r**es**
abl.	port**u**	pórt**ibus**	r**e**	r**ebus**

♦ 1st and 2nd declension adjectives can modify nouns of the 1st-5th declensions. In each example below, the adjective agrees with its noun in gender, number and case, but not declension.

	Masc.	*Fem.*	*Neuter*
Nominative S.	**pater bonus**	**mater bona**	**nomen bonum**
	good father	*good mother*	*good name*
Accusative S.	**magnum exércitum**	**magnam fidem**	**magnum bellum**
	great army	*great faith*	*great war*

♦ If the genitive singular is **-is** the noun is 3rd declension. If the genitive singular is **-ūs**, the noun is 4th declension. If the genitive singular is **-ei**, the noun is 5th declension.

♦ The direct object of a verb is in the accusative case.

68

---

2 **GRAMMAR - CHALK TALK**
What is an adjective? (a word that modifies a noun or pronoun) In Latin an adjective agrees with its noun in what three attributes? (gender, number, and case) Do an adjective and noun have to belong to the same declension? (No) What is the name of the adjectives that you learned in Lesson 18? (1st/2nd declension adjectives)

Class exercise: Write these words on the board and ask students to give the correct form of the adjective **bonus -a -um**. First have students give dictionary form and gender for each noun.

	Nom. S.	Nom. Pl.	Acc. S.	Acc. Pl.
father frater fratris m.	bonus	boni	bonum	bonos
mother mater matris f.	bona	bonae	bonam	bonas
slave servus -i m.	bonus	boni	bonum	bonos
war bellum -i n.	bonum	bona	bonum	bona
day dies -ei m.	bonus	boni	bonum	bonos
law lex legis f.	bona	bonae	bonam	bonas
land terra -ae f.	bona	bonae	bonam	bonas
farmer agrícola -ae m.	bonus	boni	bonum	bonos
heart cor cordis n.	bonum	bona	bonum	bona
fruit fructus -ūs, m.	bonus	boni	bonum	bonos

Vocabulary Review

adventus -ūs m.	*arrival*		**mater matris f.**	*mother*
canis canis m., f.	*dog*		**metus -ūs m.**	*fear*
caput cápitis n.	*head*		**miles mílitis m.**	*soldier*
cor cordis n.	*heart*		**mos moris m.**	*custom*
crux crucis f.	*cross*		**nomen nóminis n.**	*name*
dies -ei m.	*day*		**panis panis m.**	*bread*
domus -ūs f.	*house, home*		**pater patris m.**	*father*
dux ducis m.	*leader*		**pax pacis f.**	*peace*
exércitus -ūs m.	*army*		**pes pedis m.**	*foot*
fácies -ei f.	*face*		**portus -ūs m.**	*harbor*
fides -ei f.	*faith, trust*		**res -ei f.**	*thing, matter, affair, business*
flumen flúminis n.	*river*		**rex regis m.**	*king*
frater fratris m.	*brother*		**senatus -ūs m.**	*senate*
fructus -ūs m.	*fruit*		**sol solis m.**	*sun*
lacus -ūs m.	*lake*		**soror sororis f.**	*sister*
lex legis f.	*law*		**spes -ei f.**	*hope*
lumen lúminis n.	*lamp*		**spíritus -ūs m.**	*spirit*
lux lucis f.	*light*		**vox vocis f.**	*voice*
manus -ūs f.	*hand*			

Latin Sayings

alma mater
Pax Romana
Rex Regum

Caput Mundi
Senatus Populúsque Romanus (S.P.Q.R.)
Carpe diem.

LESSON XXVIII

1 **ORAL RECITATION/REVIEW**
Greeting
Teacher: *Recitemus*

> **personal & tense endings**
> **1st conj. p.p. endings**
> **amo** - six tenses, p.p.
> **do, sto, juvo, lavo** - p.p.
> **sum** - six tenses, p.p.
> **case names**
> **mensa, ae**
> **servus, i**
> **bellum, i**
> **pater, patris**
> **nomen, nóminis**
> **portus, ūs**
> **res, rei**
> **bonus -a -um**
> **unus, duo ...**
> **primus, secundus ...**

Grammar Review Questions: 1-107

LESSON XXVIII

UNITS III AND IV REVIEW

The Five Declensions

Case	1st Declension S.	Pl.	2nd Declension Masc. S.	Pl.	2nd Declension Neuter S.	Pl.
nom.	mens**a**	mens**ae**	serv**us**	serv**i**	bell**um**	bell**a**
gen.	mens**ae**	mens**arum**	serv**i**	serv**orum**	bell**i**	bell**orum**
dat.	mens**ae**	mens**is**	serv**o**	serv**is**	bell**o**	bell**is**
acc.	mens**am**	mens**as**	serv**um**	serv**os**	bell**um**	bell**a**
abl.	mens**ā**	mens**is**	serv**o**	serv**is**	bell**o**	bell**is**

Case	3rd Declension M/F S.	Pl.	3rd Declension Neuter S.	Pl.
nom.	pater	patr**es**	nomen	nómin**a**
gen.	patr**is**	patr**um**	nómin**is**	nómin**um**
dat.	patr**i**	pátr**ibus**	nómin**i**	nomín**ibus**
acc.	patr**em**	patr**es**	nomen	nómin**a**
abl.	patr**e**	pátr**ibus**	nómin**e**	nomín**ibus**

Case	4th Declension S.	Pl.	5th Declension S.	Pl.
nom.	port**us**	port**ūs**	r**es**	r**es**
gen.	port**ūs**	pórt**uum**	r**ei**	r**erum**
dat.	pórt**ui**	pórt**ibus**	r**ei**	r**ebus**
acc.	port**um**	port**ūs**	r**em**	r**es**
abl.	port**u**	pórt**ibus**	r**e**	r**ebus**

70

---

2 **GRAMMAR - CHALK TALK**
Mastery of the major paradigms of the 5 declensions is vital to success in Latin. There is no place in Latin for 'sort of' or 'halfway' knowing declensions and conjugations. The goal for this lesson is that students demonstrate mastery of the declensions, case endings, and vocabulary by completing the charts in the workbook from memory and without error. Make several copies of the workbook charts for each student and give pretests to assess student mastery. Have students study and redo these charts until they can do them without errors.

Immediate recognition of forms is a second goal for mastery learning. It is much easier to recite a declension or conjugation than it is to recognize an individual form immediately, and even harder to go from Latin to English in form drills.

Mastery must proceed in steps:
Step 1: Mastery of paradigms and vocabulary
Step 2: Ability to conjugate any verb or decline any noun according to memorized paradigms
Step 3: Rapid translation of Latin forms into English
Step 4: Rapid translation of English forms into Latin

Vocabulary Review: Units III and IV

adventus -ūs m. *arrival*	fílius -i m. *son*	panis panis m. *bread*
aeternus -a -um *eternal, everlasting*	flumen flúminis n. *river*	parvus -a -um *small*
agnus -i m. *lamb*	forum -i n. *forum, marketplace*	pater patris m. *father*
agrícola -ae m. *farmer*	frater fratris m. *brother*	pax pacis f. *peace*
altus -a -um *high, deep*	fructus -ūs m. *fruit*	pes pedis m. *foot*
amicus -i m. *friend*	Itália -ae f. *Italy*	poeta -ae m. *poet*
annus -i m. *year*	lacus -ūs m. *lake*	portus -ūs m. *harbor*
bellum -i n. *war*	latus -a -um *wide, broad*	puella -ae f. *girl*
bonus -a -um *good*	lex legis f. *law*	regina -ae f. *queen*
caelum -i n. *sky, heaven*	lumen lúminis n. *lamp*	regnum -i n. *kingdom*
canis canis m. f. *dog*	lux lucis f. *light*	res -ei f. *thing, matter,*
caput cápitis n. *head*	magnus -a -um *great, large*	*affair, business*
Christus -i m. *Christ*	malus -a -um *bad*	rex regis m. *king*
cor cordis n. *heart*	manus -ūs f. *hand*	Roma -ae f. *Rome*
crux crucis f. *cross*	Maria -ae f. *Mary*	sanctus -a -um *sacred, holy*
débitum -i n. *debt, sin*	mater matris f. *mother*	saxum -i n. *rock*
deus -i m. *god*	mensa -ae f. *table*	senatus -ūs m. *senate*
dies -ei m. *day*	metus -ūs m. *fear*	servus -i m. *slave, servant*
dóminus -i m. *lord, master*	miles mílitis m. *soldier*	sol solis m. *sun*
domus -ūs f. *house, home*	mos moris m. *custom*	soror sororis f. *sister*
donum -i n. *gift*	multus -a -um *much, many*	spes -ei f. *hope*
dux ducis m. *leader*	mundus -i m. *world, mankind*	spíritus -ūs m. *spirit*
equus -i m. *horse*	nauta -ae m. *sailor*	templum -i n. *temple*
exércitus -ūs m. *army*	nomen nóminis n. *name*	terra -ae f. *earth, land*
fácies -ei f. *face*	novus -a -um *new*	verbum -i n. *word*
fides -ei f. *faith, trust*	óppidum -i n. *town*	vox vocis f. *voice*

71

MILESTONE MARKER 3

Congratulations. You have reached another important milestone in your study of Latin. Being able to recite all five declensions (seven model nouns) is a tremendous accomplishment that you have achieved in only (15 ?) short weeks. There are many people who study Latin for years that cannot recite all five declensions as well as you! In fact I would say nearly all! In most Latin textbooks the five declensions are scattered throughout the text, which makes it hard to pull them all together and remember them. You will never have that problem!

And there is more good news! Unlike verbs there really isn't much left to learn about noun declensions. There are a few little variations in some of the five declensions, but now that you know the rules, you will be able to learn these minor variations with hardly a blink of an eye!

And now back to verbs. You will be amazed how easy it is to learn the 2nd Conjugation, your next Milestone Marker.

UNIT V INTRODUCTION

- ◆ The 1st and 2nd Conjugations are very similar.

- ◆ The Present System consists of the three tenses built on the **present stem**: the present tense, the imperfect tense, and the future tense.

- ◆ The present stem is found by dropping the **re** from the 2nd Conjugation infinitive ending, **ēre**. The stem vowel of the 2nd conjugation is **ē.**

- ◆ The Perfect System consists of the three tenses built on the perfect stem: the perfect tense, the pluperfect tense, and future perfect tense. The perfect stem is found by dropping the **i** from the 3rd principal part.

- ◆ The tense endings for the 1st and 2nd conjugations are identical.

- ◆ The 3rd and 4th conjugations are similar and will be studied in Second Form.

- ◆ Verbs are classified into conjugations by the infinitive.

Conjugation	Infinitive ending
1st	**-are**
2nd	**-ēre**
3rd	**-ere**
4th	**-ire**

72

UNIT V

Verbs
2nd Conjugation
Present And Perfect Systems

The Pantheon

Marcus Agrippa built and dedicated the original Pantheon after the Battle of Actium (31 B.C.) as a temple to all the gods of Rome. The original building was destroyed by fire and was rebuilt by the emperor Hadrian in the 2nd century. It is the best preserved of Rome's ancient buildings and survives largely because it has never been out of use—it was converted to a church in the 7th century. Today it faces one of the most popular piazzas in Rome.

73

LESSON XXIX

1 ORAL RECITATION/REVIEW

Greeting

Teacher: *Recitemus*

> **personal & tense endings**
> **1st conj. p.p. endings**
> **amo** - six tenses, p.p.
> **do, sto, juvo, lavo** - p.p.
> **sum** - six tenses, p.p.
> **case names**
> **mensa, ae**
> **servus, i**
> **bellum, i**
> **pater, patris**
> **nomen, nóminis**
> **portus, ūs**
> **res, rei**
> **bonus -a -um**
> **unus, duo ...**
> **primus, secundus ...**

Grammar Review Questions: 1-107

2 LATIN SAYING

Say aloud and ask students to repeat after you.

vídeo -ēre *verb*	to see
et *conj.*	and
táceo -ēre *verb*	to be silent

Vídeo et táceo.   *I see and am silent.*

Second Conjugation - Present Tense

Person	Singular		Plural	
1st	móne**o**	I warn	mone**mus**	we warn
2nd	mone**s**	you warn	mone**tis**	you warn
3rd	mone**t**	he, she, it warns	mone**nt**	they warn

♦ **Móneo** is the model verb chosen to illustrate the *2nd Conjugation*. All verbs in the vocabulary list are conjugated like **móneo**.

♦ The infinitive of **móneo** is **monēre**. The infinitive ending is **ēre**. All verbs whose infinitive ends in **ēre** are 2nd conjugation verbs. The **ē** of the infinitive is marked with a macron to distinguish it from the 3rd conjugation infinitive (not covered in this text).

♦ To find the present stem of a 2nd conjugation verb, drop the **re** from the infinitive.

monēre	monē/re	stem = monē

Vocabulary

débeo -ēre	to owe, ought	*debt*
dóceo -ēre*	to teach	*docile*
gáudeo -ēre*	to rejoice	*gaudy*
hábeo -ēre	to have	*habit*
móneo -ēre	to warn	*monitor*
móveo -ēre*	to move	*movable*
sédeo -ēre*	to sit	*sedate*
táceo -ēre	to be silent	*taciturn*
téneo -ēre*	to hold	*tentacle*
vídeo -ēre*	to see	*video*

* Irregular principal parts; see Lessons 31-32

74

---

4 GRAMMAR - CHALK TALK

The first two conjugations are very similar. You will find the 2nd conjugation very easy to learn. Look at this vocabulary list and compare it to the 1st conjugation verbs in Lesson 4. (2nd conjugation verbs end in **eo** and the infinitive is **ēre**.) How do you find the present stem of a verb? (Drop **re** from the infinitive) What is the stem of **móneo**? (**mone**) Write **mone** on the board six times. Ask for the endings, and write beside the stems. How does the present tense of **móneo** compare to the present tense of **amo**? (The stem vowel is **ē** instead of **a**. The 1st person singular retains the stem vowel in **móneo**, but **amo** does not have the stem vowel **a**.)

Recite *in choro* several times. (It is a little awkward at first going from 3 syllables to 2 in the first two forms, **móneo, mones**.)

Memorize the present tense of *móneo* and the meanings.

Use the *Disappearing Line Technique* as described in the Teaching Guidelines.

Word Study ◆ Grammar ◆ Syntax

◆ The stem vowel of the 2nd conjugation is **ē.** The present tense is formed by adding the personal endings to the present stem **monē**. Notice that the 1st person singular form **moneo** retains the stem vowel **e**, rather than losing it like the 1st conjugation **amo.**

◆ The complementary infinitive is often used with **débeo.** The infinitive may precede or follow the main verb. See *Sentence Pattern #2*, page 97.

Ambulare débeo.	I ought to walk.
Debes sedēre.	You ought to sit.

Vídeo et táceo. The classic statement of discretion, this saying is attributed to Queen Elizabeth I, daughter of Henry VIII. A monarch must be discreet, reasonably merciful, and not judge everything that she sees. And yet, there is an undertone of irony and even threat in this statement: "Mind you, I do see everything."

Oral Drill

hsi owes	1. **debet**	1. we are silent	tacemus
I sit	2. **sédeo**	2. they owe	debent
you (p) warn	3. **monetis**	3. I move	móveo
you teach	4. **doces**	4. she sees	videt
they hold	5. **tenent**	5. you warn	mones
hsi sees	6. **videt**	6. he has	habet
we rejoice	7. **gaudemus**	7. we hold	tenemus
I am silent	8. **táceo**	8. you ought	debes
they move	9. **movent**	9. I rejoice	gáudeo
hsi has	10. **habet**	10. they are sitting	sedent

75

VOCABULARY

Say each verb aloud with its infinitive form and meaning. Have students repeat after you.

Pronunciation helps:
soft **c** is **/ch/**
au as in *out*

Derivatives:
> debtor
> document, doctrine, indoctrinate
> admonish
> movie, remove, motion
> sedentary, sediment
> tenacious, tenant
> evident, vision

GRAMMAR - CHALK TALK

Look in Lesson 7. What is the complementary infinitive? (when an infinitive is used to complete the action of a main verb) What verb in this lesson often takes a complementary infinitive? (**débeo**)

NOTE: Even though the stem vowel is long in the 2nd conjugation, it is *not* always long in its conjugated forms. Students should be required to add the macron for the infinitive form only.

LESSON XXX

1 **ORAL RECITATION/REVIEW**
Greeting
Teacher: *Recitemus*

      personal & tense endings
      1st conj. p.p. endings
      amo - six tenses, p.p.
      do, sto, juvo, lavo - p.p.
      sum - six tenses, p.p.
      case names
      mensa, ae
      servus, i
      bellum, i
      pater, patris
      nomen, nóminis
      portus,ūs
      res, rei
      bonus -a -um
      unus, duo ...
      primus, secundus ...
      móneo - present tense

Grammar Review Questions: 1-107

2 **LATIN SAYING**
Say aloud and ask students to repeat after you.

cáveo -ēre   to beware of
  cave *imperative mood*
canis canis *m./f.*   dog
  canem *acc. case*

LESSON XXX

Cave canem.   *Beware the dog.*

Second Conjugation - Imperfect and Future Tenses

Imperfect			
mone**bam**	I was warning	mone**bamus**	we were warning
mone**bas**	you were warning	mone**batis**	you were warning
mone**bat**	he, she, it was warning	mone**bant**	they were warning

Future			
mone**bo**	I will warn	moné**bimus**	we will warn
mone**bis**	you will warn	moné**bitis**	you will warn
mone**bit**	he, she, it will warn	mone**bunt**	they will warn

◆ The imperfect and future tense endings are identical to those of the 1st conjugation.

Vocabulary

appáreo -ēre	to appear	*appearance*
árdeo -ēre*	to burn, be on fire	*arson*
cáveo -ēre*	to beware of, guard against	*caution*
júbeo -ēre*	to order, command	
máneo -ēre*	to remain, stay	*mansion*
prohíbeo -ēre	to prevent	*prohibit*
respóndeo -ēre*	to respond, answer	*response*
térreo -ēre	to frighten	*terrify*
tímeo -ēre*	to fear, be afraid of	*timid*
váleo -ēre*	to be strong, be well	*valor*

* Irregular principal parts; see Lessons 31-32

76

---

4 **GRAMMAR - CHALK TALK**
What are the three tenses of the Present System? (present, imperfect, future) All three tenses of the Present System are built on what stem? (the present stem) How do you find the present stem? (drop **re** from the infinitive) What is the infinitive ending of the 1st conjugation? (**are**) of the 2nd conjugation? (**ēre**) What differences are there between the 1st and 2nd conjugation tense endings? (There aren't any) What is the stem vowel of the 1st conjugation? (**a**) of the 2nd conjugation? (**e**) What kind of past action does the imperfect tense describe? (an ongoing, repeated or interrupted action in the past) What does *imperfect* mean in Latin? (incomplete)

Class practice: Find the stem of **cáveo** and **respóndeo** and conjugate in the present system.

        Memorize the imperfect and future tenses of *móneo* and the meanings.

Use the *Disappearing Line Technique* as described in the Teaching Guidelines.

Word Study ♦ Grammar ♦ Syntax

♦ **Tímeo** is often used with the complementary infinitive. See *Sentence Pattern #2*, page 97.

Pugnare tímeo.	**Timemus natare.**
to fight I am afraid	*we fear to swim*
I am afraid to fight.	We fear to swim.

> **Cave canem** was as familiar a phrase to the ancient Romans as it is to us. Many Roman houses had the image of a ferocious dog portrayed in mosaic at the front entrance.

Oral Drill

hsi was owing	1. **debebat**	1. I will warn	monebo
I will be well	2. **valebo**	2. you were frightening	terrebas
they will have	3. **habebunt**	3. they will respond	respondebunt
we prevent	4. **prohibemus**	4. we are being silent	tacemus
you frighten	5. **terres**	5. you will appear	apparebis
they were appearing	6. **apparebant**	6. it was preventing	prohibebat
they are silent	7. **tacent**	7. I was being silent	tacebam
you (p) will warn	8. **monébitis**	8. they ought	debent
hsi will owe	9. **debebit**	9. we appear	apparemus
they were having	10. **habebant**	10. she has	habet

77

VOCABULARY ③

Say each verb aloud with its infinitive form and meaning. Have students repeat after you.

Students confuse
térreo and **tímeo**
móneo, **máneo**, and **móveo**.

Pronunciation helps:
j is pronounced like **y** in *yes*

Derivatives:
> *caveat*
> *prohibition*
> *apparent*
> *valid, valiant, valuable*
> *terrific*
> *intimidate*

GRAMMAR - CHALK TALK

What is the complementary infinitive? (an infinitive used to complete the action of the main verb) What verb in this lesson is often followed by a complementary infinitive? (**tímeo**) in the previous lesson? (**débeo**) What three 1st conjugation verbs may be followed by a complementary infinitive? (**paro, amo, opto**)

LESSON XXXI

1 **ORAL RECITATION/REVIEW**
Greeting
Teacher: *Recitemus*

    personal & tense endings
    1st conj. p.p. endings
    amo - six tenses, p.p.
    do, sto, juvo, lavo - p.p.
    sum - six tenses, p.p.
    móneo - three tenses
    case names
    mensa, ae
    servus, i
    bellum, i
    pater, patris
    nomen, nóminis
    portus, ūs
    res, rei
    bonus -a -um
    unus, duo ...
    primus, secundus ...

Grammar Review Questions: 1-108

2 **LATIN SAYING**
Say aloud and ask students to repeat after you.

docēre	to teach
delectare	to delight
movēre	to move

What is the conjugation of **delectare**? (1st) How do you know? (The infinitive ending is -**are**.)

LESSON XXXI

Docēre, delectare, movēre
To teach, to delight, to move

Second Conjugation   Principal Parts

1st	2nd	3rd	4th
món eo	mon ēre	món ui	món itus
I warn	to warn	I warned	warned
eo	**ēre**	**ui**	**itus**

♦ The regular principal parts with regular endings for the 2nd conjugation are given above. Notice the similarities and differences with the 1st conjugation principal parts.

♦ In a vocabulary list or dictionary entry, a verb that is followed by **(2)** or **ēre**, has regular principal parts. If the principal parts are irregular, they will be written out in full.

♦ To write the principal parts of regular 2nd conjugation verbs, drop the eo from the first principal part and add the regular endings **ēre, ui, itus.**

Second Conjugation - Present System

Present Tense	
móne o	mone mus
mone s	mone tis
mone t	mone nt

Imperfect Tense	
mone bam	mone bamus
mone bas	mone batis
mone bat	mone bant

Future Tense	
mone bo	moné bimus
mone bis	moné bitis
mone bit	mone bunt

78

---

3 **GRAMMAR - CHALK TALK**

What is the purpose of principal parts? (to find the stems) Write the regular endings for the 1st conjugation principal parts on the board and the regular endings for the 2nd principal parts underneath. Compare and contrast. Say the 2nd conjugation regular endings *in choro* several times. Going around the room, ask students to give the principal parts of all of the verbs with regular principal parts listed in **Bullet 3**.

Many 2nd conjugation verbs have irregular principal parts. Irregular principal parts are a real stumbling block for students. The only way to master them is to say them aloud over and over. Write the principal parts of each of the verbs below, one at a time, and have students identify the irregularity.

tímeo	no 4th part	
váleo	no 4th part	
dóceo	4th part missing letter **i**	
téneo	4th part missing letter **i**	
árdeo	**d** in root changes to **s**	endings are **i** and **us**, instead of **ui** and **itus**
júbeo	**b** in root changes to **ss**	endings are **i** and **us**, instead of **ui** and **itus**
máneo	letter **s** added to root	endings are **i** and **us**, instead of **ui** and **itus**

◆ Say each verb with its regular principal parts.

móneo (2)	*to warn*
appáreo (2)	*to appear*
débeo (2)	*to owe, ought*
hábeo (2)	*to have*
prohíbeo (2)	*to prevent*
térreo (2)	*to frighten*
táceo (2)	*to be silent*

◆ These verbs have irregular principal parts. Each one must be learned individually. Say each one aloud many times, until you know them all perfectly.

1st	2nd	3rd	4th
tímeo	timēre	tímui	--
váleo	valēre	válui	--
dóceo	docēre	dócui	doctus
téneo	tenēre	ténui	tentus
árdeo	ardēre	arsi	arsus
júbeo	jubēre	jussi	jussus
máneo	manēre	mansi	mansus

Docēre, delectare, movēre is a paraphrase of one of Quintilian's principles of oratory. The speaker should not only instruct his audience, but move them and delight them as well. The triplet was used by St. Augustine and by many rhetoricians of the Renaissance. It is the motto of *Highlands Latin School* in Louisville, Kentucky.

79

GRAMMAR - CHALK TALK

④

Say the principal parts of these verbs aloud *in choro* several times, and then have individual students say a verb's principal parts aloud.

****Memorize the regular principal parts of *móneo* and
the irregular principal parts of all verbs listed in this lesson.****

You must say these irregular principal parts aloud *every day* with your students until you and they know them perfectly. The only way to learn principal parts is to say them aloud many, many times. It is also important to write them occasionally to check spelling.

LESSON XXXII

① ORAL RECITATION/REVIEW
Greeting
Teacher: *Recitemus*

> **personal & tense endings**
> **1st conj. p.p. endings**
> **amo** - six tenses, p.p.
> **do, sto, juvo, lavo** - p.p.
> **sum** - six tenses, p.p.
> **móneo** - three tenses, pp.
> **(tímeo, váleo, dóceo, téneo,**
> **árdeo, júbeo, máneo)** - p.p.
> **case names**
> **mensa, ae**
> **servus, i**
> **bellum, i**
> **pater, patris**
> **nomen, nóminis**
> **portus, ūs**
> **res, rei**
> **bonus -a -um**
> **unus, duo ...**
> **primus, secundus ...**

Grammar Review Questions: 1-110

② LATIN SAYING
Say aloud and ask students to repeat after you.

vénio *4th conj.*		to come
vídeo *2nd conj.*		to see
vinco *3rd conj.*		to conquer

LESSON XXXII

Veni, vidi, vici.   *I came, I saw, I conquered.*

Second Conjugation - Perfect System

Perfect			
mónu i	I have warned	**monú imus**	we have warned
monu isti	you have warned	**monu istis**	you have warned
mónu it	hsi has warned	**monu erunt**	they have warned
Pluperfect			
monú eram	I had warned	**monu eramus**	we had warned
monú eras	you had warned	**monu eratis**	you had warned
monú erat	hsi had warned	**monú erant**	they had warned
Future Perfect			
monú ero	I will have warned	**monu érimus**	we will have warned
monú eris	you will have warned	**monu éritis**	you will have warned
monú erit	hsi will have warned	**monu erint**	they will have warned

♦ These verbs have irregular principal parts. Each one must be learned individually. Say each one aloud until you know them all perfectly.

1st	2nd	3rd	4th
gáudeo*	gaudēre	--	--
cáveo	cavēre	cavi	cautus
sédeo	sedēre	sedi	sessus
vídeo	vidēre	vidi	visus
respóndeo	respondēre	respondi	responsus
móveo	movēre	movi	motus

***Gáudeo** is irregular in the perfect system.

All three verbs are the 1st person
singular of the perfect tense, which is also the 3rd principal part.

③ GRAMMAR - CHALK TALK
What three tenses make up the Present System? (present, imperfect, future) the Perfect System? (perfect, pluperfect, future perfect) The Present System is built on what stem? (the present stem) How do you find the present stem? (Drop **re** from the infinitive.) How do you find the perfect stem? (Drop **i** from the 3rd principal part.)
What are the perfect tense endings? (**-i, -isti, -it, -imus, -istis, -erunt**) the pluperfect tense endings? (imperfect tense of **sum: -eram, -eras, -erat, -eramus, -eratis, -erant**) the future perfect tense endings? (**-ero, -eris, -erit, -erimus, -eritis, -erint**) What are the future perfect tense endings similar to? (the future of **sum**, except for the 3rd P Pl.)

Look at the conjugation of the perfect system of **móneo**. How does it compare to the perfect system of the 1st conjugation? (It is built on the perfect stem and the tense endings are the same.) Recite *in choro*.

Memorize the Perfect System of *móneo*.

Use the *Disappearing Line Technique* as described in the Teaching Guidelines.

Word Study • Grammar • Syntax

- The Perfect System consists of three tenses: perfect, pluperfect, and future perfect.
- The Perfect System is built on the perfect stem.
- To find the perfect stem drop the personal ending **i** from the 3rd principal part.

móneo monēre mónui mónitus

monu/i = monu

- The tense endings for the perfect system of the 2nd conjugation are identical to those of the 1st conjugation, as are the meanings.

Julius Caesar

Veni, vidi, vici. In 47 B.C., Julius Caesar defeated the king of Pontus in one hour. He was so proud of his extraordinary speed that he sent the famous message to the Senate in Rome: **veni vidi vici**. A successful general was allowed to have a victory parade, called a *triumph*. There was a grand procession along the Via Sacra in the Forum in which the general showed off his prisoners, the spoils of victory, and displays relating to the events of the campaign. Caesar's Pontic triumph was unusual in that the central place was given to a placard bearing the simple inscription

VENI VIDI VICI.

81

GRAMMAR - CHALK TALK

④

How many 1st conjugation verbs did you learn in Unit I? (50) How many of these verbs had irregular principal parts? (4) Name them. (**do, sto, lavo, juvo**) How many 2nd conjugation verbs have you learned? (20) How many have regular principal parts? (7) How many have irregular principal parts? (13) Learning irregular principal parts is a challenge. The only way to remember them is to say them aloud over and over. Remember the first two principal parts are always regular. It is only the last two that you have to work on. Look at the 3rd principal part of these verbs. Can you see one way they are similar? (the 3rd principal part of each verb has the same form, the root plus the ending i. The 4th principal part of these verbs is quite irregular. Recite *in choro* several times and individually around the room.

Memorize the irregular principal parts of all verbs listed in this lesson.

You must say these irregular principal parts aloud *every day* with your students until you and they know them perfectly. The only way to learn principal parts is to say them aloud many, many times. It is also important to write them occasionally to check spelling.

LESSON XXXIII

1 **ORAL RECITATION/REVIEW**
Greeting
Teacher: *Recitemus*

> **personal & tense endings**
> **1st conj. p.p. endings**
> **amo** - six tenses, p.p.
> **do, sto, juvo, lavo** - p.p.
> **sum** - six tenses, p.p.
> **móneo** - six tenses, pp.
> **(tímeo, váleo, dóceo, téneo,**
> **árdeo, júbeo, máneo,**
> **gáudeo, cáveo, respóndeo,**
> **vídeo, sédeo, móveo)** - p.p.
> **case names**
> **mensa, ae**
> **servus, i**
> **bellum, i**
> **pater, patris**
> **nomen, nóminis**
> **portus, ūs**
> **res, rei**
> **bonus -a -um**
> **unus, duo ...**
> **primus, secundus ...**

Grammar Review Questions: 1-110

Second Conjugation   Indicative Active
present stem: **monē-**

Present	
móne o	mone mus
mone s	mone tis
mone t	mone nt
Imperfect	
mone bam	mone bamus
mone bas	mone batis
mone bat	mone bant
Future	
mone bo	moné bimus
mone bis	moné bitis
mone bit	mone bunt

perfect stem: **monu-**

Perfect	
mónu i	monú imus
monu isti	monu istis
mónu it	monu erunt
Pluperfect	
monú eram	monu eramus
monú eras	monu eratis
monú erat	monu erant
Future Perfect	
monú ero	monu érimus
monú eris	monu éritis
monú erit	monu erint

82

2 **GRAMMAR - CHALK TALK**
The purpose of this lesson is to review and bring together the knowledge and understanding of the Second Conjugation and especially the 13 verbs with irregular principal parts.

Vocabulary Review

móneo (2)	*to warn*
appáreo (2)	*to appear*
débeo (2)	*to owe, ought*
hábeo (2)	*to have*
prohíbeo (2)	*to prevent*
térreo (2)	*to frighten*
táceo (2)	*to be silent*

1st	2nd	3rd	4th	Meaning
tímeo	**timēre**	**tímui**	—	*to fear, be afraid of*
váleo	**valēre**	**válui**	—	*to be strong, be well*
dóceo	**docēre**	**dócui**	**doctus**	*to teach*
téneo	**tenēre**	**ténui**	**tentus**	*to hold*
árdeo	**ardēre**	**arsi**	**arsus**	*to burn, be on fire*
júbeo	**jubēre**	**jussi**	**jussus**	*to order, command*
máneo	**manēre**	**mansi**	**mansus**	*to remain, stay*
gáudeo	**gaudēre**	—	—	*to rejoice*
cáveo	**cavēre**	**cavi**	**cautus**	*to beware of, guard against*
sédeo	**sedēre**	**sedi**	**sessus**	*to sit*
vídeo	**vidēre**	**vidi**	**visus**	*to see*
respóndeo	**respondēre**	**respondi**	**responsus**	*to respond, answer*
móveo	**movēre**	**movi**	**motus**	*to move*

Latin Sayings

Vídeo et táceo.
Cave canem.

Docēre, delectare, movēre
Veni, vidi, vici.

83

LESSON XXXIV

ORAL RECITATION/REVIEW
Greeting
Teacher: *Recitemus*

personal & tense endings
1st conj. p.p. endings
amo - six tenses, p.p.
do, sto, juvo, lavo - p.p.
sum - six tenses, p.p.
móneo - six tenses, pp.
(tímeo, váleo, dóceo, téneo,
árdeo, júbeo, máneo,
gáudeo, cáveo, respóndeo,
vídeo, sédeo, móveo) - p.p.
case names
mensa, ae
servus, i
bellum, i
pater, patris
nomen, nóminis
portus, ūs
res, rei
bonus -a -um
unus, duo ...
primus, secundus ...

Grammar Review Questions: 1-110

LESSON XXXIV
Verb Review - Units I, II, and V

Tense	Number	1st Conjugation	2nd Conjugation	Sum
Present	sing.	amo	móneo	sum
		amas	mones	es
		amat	monet	est
	pl.	amamus	monemus	sumus
		amatis	monetis	estis
		amant	monent	sunt
Imperfect	sing.	amabam	monebam	eram
		amabas	monebas	eras
		amabat	monebat	erat
	pl.	amabamus	monebamus	eramus
		amabatis	monebatis	eratis
		amabant	monebant	erant
Future	sing.	amabo	monebo	ero
		amabis	monebis	eris
		amabit	monebit	erit
	pl.	amábimus	monébimus	érimus
		amábitis	monébitis	éritis
		amabunt	monebunt	erunt
Perfect	sing.	amavi	mónui	fui
		amavisti	monuisti	fuisti
		amavit	mónuit	fuit
	pl.	amávimus	monúimus	fúimus
		amavistis	monuistis	fuistis
		amaverunt	monuerunt	fuerunt
Pluperfect	sing.	amáveram	monúeram	fúeram
		amáveras	monúeras	fúeras
		amáverat	monúerat	fúerat
	pl.	amaveramus	monueramus	fueramus
		amaveratis	monueratis	fueratis
		amáverant	monúerant	fúerant
Future perfect	sing.	amávero	monúero	fúero
		amáveris	monúeris	fúeris
		amáverit	monúerit	fúerit
	pl.	amavérimus	monuérimus	fuérimus
		amavéritis	monuéritis	fuéritis
		amáverint	monúerint	fúerint

84

MILESTONE MARKER 4
Congratulations on completing *First Form Latin*. You have accomplished much and can look back on your year of Latin with pride and amazement. Did you ever think you could learn this much in one year? After reviewing and completing this lesson take time for a celebration.

Continue to review all you have learned over the summer. Do your oral recitation at least twice each week. Work on your flashcards a little each day.

In the fall you will be ready for the next segment of our journey. You will be tested and challenged again. But you will be ready - because this year, you have learned how to learn with Latin. You are tough, you are in shape, you have what it takes to climb the mountain of Latin to the very top!

FIRST - SECOND CONJUGATION VERBS

accuso (1)	to accuse	narro (1)	to tell
adoro (1)	to adore	nato (1)	to swim
ámbulo (1)	to walk	návigo (1)	to sail
amo (1)	to love, like	nego (1)	to deny
appáreo (2)	to appear	núntio (1)	to report
appello (1)	to address	óccupo (1)	to seize
árdeo -ēre arsi arsus	to burn, be on fire	oppugno (1)	to attack
aro (1)	to plow	opto (1)	to desire, wish
cáveo -ēre cavi cautus	to beware of, guard against	oro (1)	to speak, pray
celo (1)	to hide	paro (1)	to prepare
clamo (1)	to shout	perturbo (1)	to disturb
creo (1)	to create	porto (1)	to carry
culpo (1)	to blame	prohíbeo (2)	to prevent
débeo (2)	to owe, ought	pugno (1)	to fight
delecto (1)	to delight, please	puto (1)	to think
demonstro (1)	to show, point out	respóndeo -ēre respondi responsus	to respond, answer
do -are dedi datus	to give	rogo (1)	to ask
dóceo -ēre dócui doctus	to teach	saluto (1)	to greet
dúbito (1)	to doubt	sédeo -ēre sedi sessus	to sit
erro (1)	to err, wander	servo (1)	to guard, keep
exploro (1)	to explore	specto (1)	to look at
exspecto (1)	to wait for, expect	spero (1)	to hope
gáudeo -ēre -- --	to rejoice	sto -are steti status	to stand
hábeo (2)	to have	súpero (1)	to overcome
hábito (1)	to live in, dwell	táceo (2)	to be silent
júbeo -ēre jussi jussus	to order, command	tempto (1)	to tempt
júdico (1)	to judge, consider	téneo -ēre ténui tentus	to hold
juvo -are juvi jutus	to help	térreo (2)	to frighten
laboro (1)	to work	tímeo -ēre timui --	to fear, be afraid of
laudo (1)	to praise	váleo -ēre válui --	to be strong, be well
lavo -are lavi lautus	to wash	vídeo -ēre vidi visus	to see
líbero (1)	to set free	voco (1)	to call
máneo -ēre mansi mansus	to remain, stay	volo (1)	to fly
móneo (2)	to warn	vúlnero (1)	to wound
móveo -ēre movi motus	to move		
muto (1)	to change	sum esse fui futurus	to be

85

APPENDICES

Everyday Latin

Salve (salvete)*	*Greetings, hello*
Vale (valete)	*Good bye*
Quid est nomen tibi?	*What is your name?*
Mihi nomen est ...	*My name is ...*
Quid agis?	*How are you?*
Váleo.	*I am well.*
Admirábilis	*Wonderful*
Grátias tibi ago.	*Thank you.*
Nihil est. (Optatus/-ata venis. [m/f])	*You are most welcome.*
Ignosce mihi, quaeso.	*Pardon (excuse) me, please.*
Sodes	*Please (would you mind, if you don't mind)*
Me paénitet.	*I'm sorry.*
Te amo.	*I love you.*
(Ego amo te.)	*I love you. (Not as correct but a student favorite)*
Ita.	*Yes.*

Classroom Latin

Salvete, amici Latinae.	*Greetings, friends of Latin.*
Salvete, discípuli.	*Hello, students.*
Salve, magister/magistra. (m/f)	*Greetings (hello), teacher.*
Salve, discípule.	*Hello, student.*
Vale, magister/magistra. (m/f)	*Good bye, teacher.*
Valete, discípuli.	*Good bye, students.*
Sede. (Sedete.)	*Sit down.*
Surge. (Súrgite.)	*Stand up.*
Adsum	*Present*
Áperi ... (Aperite ...)	*Open*
Claude ... (Cláudite ...)	*Close*
jánuam	*door*
fenestram, fenestras	*window, windows*
librum, libros	*book, books*

*The words in parentheses are plural commands or greetings.

Audi (Audite) diligenter.	*Listen carefully.*
Impossíbile est.	*That is impossible.*
Esne confusus/confusa? *(m/f)*	*Are you puzzled?*
Éxplica, quaeso.	*Please explain.*
Non intéllego.	*I don't understand.*
Ádjuva (adjuvate) me.	*Help me.*
Fallit.	*It is wrong.*
Falsus	*Wrong, incorrect*
Verum	*Correct*
Siléntium, quaeso	*Silence, please*
Tace. (Tacete.)	*Be silent.*
Ad páginam ...	*Turn to page ...*
Responde mihi.	*Answer me.*
Oremus.	*Let us pray.*
Bene actum.	*Well done.*
Óptime!	*Excellent!*
Péssime!	*Very bad!*
Scribe (scríbite) haec verba.	*Write these words.*
Fiat.	*All right (let it be done).*
De hoc satis!	*Enough of this!*
Cóllige fólia.	*Collect the papers.*
Quid dixit? dixisti?	*What did he say? you say?*

Signum Crucis

In nómine Patris et Fílii et Spíritus Sancti.

Pater Noster

Pater Noster, Qui es in Caelis. Sanctificetur Nomen Tuum. Advéniat Regnum Tuum, fiat voluntas Tua, sicut in Caelo et in terra. Panem nostrum cotidianum da nobis hódie. Et dimitte nobis débita nostra, sicut et nos dimíttimus debitóribus nostris, et ne nos inducas in tentationem, sed líbera nos a malo.

Table Blessing

Benedíc Dómine nos et haec tua dona quae de tua largitate sumus sumpturi.

Per Christum Dóminum Nostrum. Amen.

Doxology (Glória Patri)

Glória Patri et Fílio et Spirítui Sancto. Sicut erat in princípio et nunc et semper et in saécula saeculorum. Amen

Sanctus and Benedictus

Sanctus, Sanctus, Sanctus, Dóminus Deus Sábaoth. Pleni sunt Caeli et terra glória Tua.

Hosanna in Excelsis. Benedictus qui venit in nómine Dómini. Hosanna in Excelsis.

Agnus Dei

Agnus Dei, qui tollis peccata mundi, miserere nobis.
Agnus Dei, qui tollis peccata mundi, miserere nobis.
Agnus Dei, qui tollis peccata mundi, dona nobis pacem.

Ave Maria

Ave Maria, grátia plena, Dóminus tecum. Benedicta tu in muliéribus, et benedictus fructus ventris tui, Jesus.

Sancta Maria, Mater Dei, ora pro nobis peccatóribus. Nunc et in hora mortis nostrae. Amen.

Sign of the Cross

In the name of the Father, the Son, and the Holy Ghost.

Our Father

Our Father, who art in Heaven. Hallowed be thy name. Thy Kingdom come, thy will be done, on earth as it is in Heaven. Give us this day our daily bread and forgive us our trespasses as we forgive those who trespass against us, and lead us not into temptation but deliver us from evil.

Table Blessing

Bless us O Lord and these thy gifts which we are about to receive from thy bounty. Through Christ Our Lord, Amen.

Doxology

Glory be to the Father, and to the Son, and to the Holy Spirit. As it was in the beginning, is now and ever shall be, world without end. Amen.

Sanctus and Benedictus

Holy, Holy, Holy, Lord God of Hosts. Heaven and earth are full of Your glory.
Hosanna in the highest. Blessed is he who comes in the name of the Lord.
Hosanna in the highest.

Agnus Dei

Lamb of God, you take away the sins of the world, have mercy on us.
Lamb of God, you take away the sins of the world, have mercy on us.
Lamb of God, you take away the sins of the world, grant us peace.

Hail Mary

Hail Mary, full of grace, The Lord is with thee, Blessed art thou among women
And blessed is the fruit of thy womb, Jesus

Holy Mary, Mother of God, Pray for us sinners,
Now and at the hour of our death. Amen.

alma mater*	*nurturing mother*
Anno Dómini (A.D.)*	*In the year of our Lord*
ante bellum*	*before the war*
Caput Mundi	*Head of the World*
Carpe diem.	*Seize the day.*
Cave canem.	*Beware the dog.*
Civis Romanus sum.	*I am a Roman citizen.*
Docēre, delectare, movēre	*To teach, to delight, to move*
Errare est humanum.	*To err is human.*
Fortes fortuna juvat.	*Fortune aids the brave.*
In choro recitemus.	*Let us recite together.*
In umbra, ígitur, pugnábimus.	*Then we will fight in the shade.*
Mater Itáliae Roma*	*The mother of Italy, Rome*
nunc aut numquam*	*now or never*
Ora et labora.*	*Pray and work.*
Pax Romana*	*The Roman Peace*
Quáttuor anni témpora	*The four seasons of the year*
Rex Regum	*King of Kings*
Roma Aeterna	*Eternal Rome*
semper fidelis*	*always faithful*
Senatus Populúsque Romanus (S.P.Q.R.)*	*The Senate and People of Rome*
Stabat Mater	*The Mother was Standing*
Veni, vidi, vici.*	*I came, I saw, I conquered.*
Vídeo et táceo.	*I see and am silent.*

*Sayings also in *Latina Christiana*

A sentence is a complete thought and is made of two basic parts, the **subject** and the **predicate**.

Mary   **walks.**

subject   predicate

The subject is **what** or **who** the sentence is about.
The predicate tells what the subject **is** or **does**.

The *complete subject* contains the subject with all of its modifiers. The *simple subject* is usually just called the subject. The *complete predicate* contains the simple predicate and its modifiers. The simple predicate is called the *verb*. Modifiers in the subject and predicate do not change the basic structure of the sentence.

simple subject   simple predicate (main verb with helping verbs)

Shouting with joy, <u>Mary</u>   <u>was skipping</u> through the garden yesterday.
complete subject   complete predicate

One way to help students understand grammar is to label each word in a sentence. Here is a list of sentence parts and their abbreviations. Students can write these abbreviations above each word and then diagram each sentence. Here are the labels that will be used in this text.

Subject noun	SN
Subject pronoun	SP
Subject (personal ending - Latin verb)	SPE
Verb	V
Verb-transitive	V-t
Linking verb	LV
Article	A
Adjective	Adj
Adverb	Adv
Predicate adjective	PA
Predicate nominative	PrN
Direct object	DO
Complementary infinitive	CI

Action Verbs

Action verbs express action, either seen, such as *do, run, write* and *go,* or unseen such as *think, believe,* and *know.*

Action verbs can be *transitive* or *intransitive.* Most verbs are transitive because they express action that can be passed from the subject to another person or thing in the sentence, the direct object.

SN   V-t   DO

Ben eats the sandwich.

Eat is a transitive verb because the action is passed from the subject to the direct object, the *sandwich.*

Some verbs, by their nature, cannot take a direct object.

Ben is sleeping. Ben will arrive late.

Sleep and *arrive* are intransitive. The action cannot be passed on to another person or thing in the sentence. (*Late* is an adverb, not a direct object.)

State of Being Verbs

A state of being verb expresses existence or state of being. It does not express action, and therefore by definition is *intransitive.*

The most common state of being verb is the *to be* verb, whose forms in English are *am, is, are, was, were, be, being, been.*

The *to be* verb is usually a linking verb, linking the subject to a word in the predicate that names or describes the subject.

SN   LV   PrN   SN LV PA

Ben was a soldier.   Ben is strong.

In these sentences, the noun that renames the subject is called the predicate nominative (PrN) and the adjective that describes the subject is called the predicate adjective (PA).

There are seven basic sentence patterns. Four will be presented in this text. Each of these sentence patterns will be labeled and diagrammed.

Diagramming

Diagramming gives students a picture of sentence structure, and is another effective technique to help students understand grammar. The diagram begins with a horizontal line that contains the backbone of the sentence—the subject and the verb. Crossing over this line is a vertical line that divides the sentence into its two parts, the simple subject on the left and the verb on the right. Adjectives and adverbs are written on slanted lines below the words they modify.

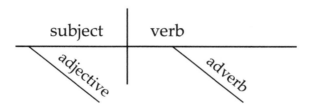

Complements are written on the horizontal line and separated from the verb by a line which <u>does not</u> cross over the base line. If the complement is a direct object, the vertical line is perpendicular to the base line.

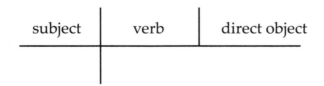

If the complement is a predicate nominative or adjective, the vertical line is slanted to the left.

subject | verb \ pred. nom   subject | verb \ pred. adj.

Sentence Pattern #1
Subject + Verb

If an action verb is intransitive, all that is needed for a sentence is the backbone—a subject and a verb. The subject can be a noun or a pronoun, and other modifiers, such as adverbs and adjectives, do not change the basic pattern.

The verb can be one word or it can be a verb phrase. A verb phrase contains a main verb plus all of its helping verbs. In this text we will underline the verb phrase when labeling sentences.

SN   V   Adv

Mary <u>is walking</u> today.

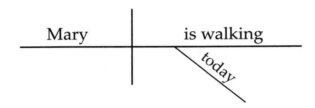

In Latin, the subject of a sentence can be the personal ending of the verb (SPE). Here is a model for diagramming and labeling this kind of sentence in both English and Latin.

V   SPE   SP   V

Ámbulo   **I walk.**

(o)	ámbulo		I	walk

Sentence Patterns #2 through #4

Sentence Pattern #1 above is the only one of the seven basic sentence patterns that does <u>not</u> have **complements**. Most verbs need a completer to *complete* their meaning. If I say *Mary likes*, you do not feel like I have finished my thought. You want to know *what Mary likes*. All of the six remaining sentence patterns have complements. We will learn three complements in this text: the *direct object, predicate nominative*, and *predicate adjective*.

Sentence Pattern #2
Subject + Verb + Direct Object

The first type of complement is the direct object. Typical English word order is *subject-verb-direct object*. Typical Latin word order is *subject-direct object-verb*. Diagramming follows English word order.

The direct object can be a noun or pronoun …

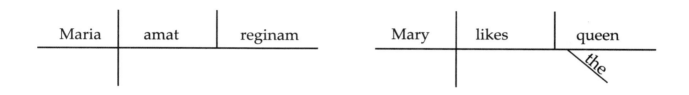

or other more complex constructions, such as the *Complementary Infinitive (CI)*.

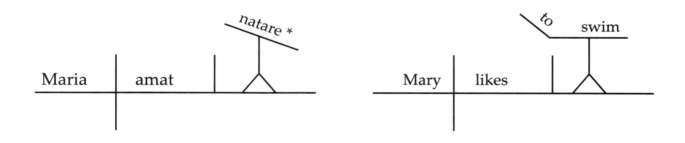

* We are using a single slanted line here because "to swim" is one word in Latin.

Sentence Pattern #3
Subject + Verb + Predicate Adjective

Verbs that are completed by a predicate nominative or adjective are called *linking verbs*. They are *intransitive* because they are not completed by a direct object. If an adjective follows the linking verb and describes the subject, it is called a *predicate adjective* and is in the nominative case.

Sentence Pattern #4
Subject + Verb + Predicate Nominative

If a noun follows the linking verb and renames the subject, it is called a *predicate nominative* and is in the nominative case.

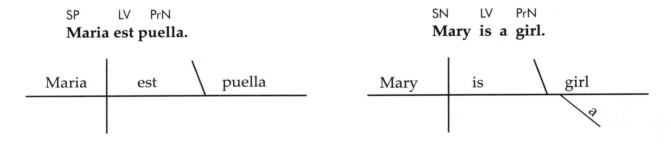

Again, modifiers do not change the basic sentence pattern.

SN   LV   Adj   PrN   Adv
Mary is a good girl today.

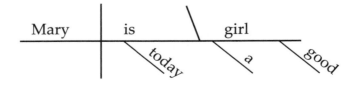

This chart provides a more detailed breakdown of specific Latin sentence patterns.

Sentence Type	Lesson Introduced	Symbols			Examples	Description
#1a	Lesson 2	SPE	V		**Ámbulat.** *She walks.*	Personal ending subject + action verb
#1b	Lesson 17	SN	V		**Maria ámbulat.** *Mary is walking. (Mary walks.)*	Noun subject + action verb
#2a	Lesson 7	SPE	V-t	CI	**Amat ambulare.** *She loves to walk.*	Personal ending subject + action verb + complementary infinitive
#2b	Lesson 17	SN	V-t	CI	**Maria ambulare amat.** *Mary loves to walk.*	Noun subject + action verb + complementary infinitive
#2c	Lesson 24	SPE	V-t	DO	**Reginam laudat.** *She praises the queen.*	Personal ending subject + action verb + direct object
#2d	Lesson 24	SN	V-t	DO	**Maria reginam laudat.** *Mary praises the queen.*	Noun subject + action verb + direct object
#3	Lesson 19	SN	LV	PA	**Maria est bona.** *Mary is good.*	Noun subject + linking verb + predicate adjective
#4	Lesson 19	SN	LV	PrN	**Maria est puella.** *Mary is a girl.*	Noun subject + linking verb + predicate nominative

Parts of Speech

Grammar is the study of how language works—how it enables humans to communicate thoughts. There are eight kinds of words, or *parts of speech*. Here is a quick way to remember them:

1. *What are the most important kinds of words?*	Nouns
2. *What words modify nouns?*	Adjectives
3. *What words take the place of nouns?*	Pronouns
4. *What are the second most important kinds of words?*	Verbs
5. *What words modify verbs?*	Adverbs
6. *What three parts of speech end with* **tion**?	Prepositions
	Conjunctions
	Interjections

Part of Speech	Definition	Examples	Latin Roots
noun	names a person, place, thing	*John, Rome, book*	**nomen**
verb	shows action or state of being	*see, think, eat*	**verbum**
adjective	modifies a noun or pronoun	*big, red, many*	**ad jácere**
adverb	modifies verb, adjective, or adverb	*quickly, now*	**ad verbum**
pronoun	takes place of noun	*I, you, who*	**pronomen**
preposition	shows relationship of a noun or pronoun to another word	*in, on, about, with*	**prae posítio**
conjunction	joins words	*and, but, or*	**con júngere**
interjection	an exclamation that is not part of sentence	*Oh! Whew!*	**inter jácere**

(*The, a,* and *an* are called *articles* and are considered adjectives.)

Words used as more than one part of speech

An individual word can be more than one part of speech depending on how it is used in a sentence.

The **total** is sixty.	*noun*
It was a **total** disaster.	*adjective*
He will **total** the score.	*verb*

Parts of a Sentence

Words are used to communicate thoughts. A sentence is a complete thought, created first in the human mind. A sentence has two parts: a subject and a predicate. The subject is what the sentence is about, and the predicate tells what the subject *is* or *does*. Every sentence, no matter how long or complicated, can be divided into these two parts:

subject	who or what the sentence is about
predicate	what the subject *is* or *does*

Example:

The pretty girl gave me a wave and a wink in the garden. Wow!

Sentence Part	Definition	Example
simple subject	who or what the sentence is about	girl
complete subject	subject and its modifiers	The pretty girl
complete predicate	tells something about subject	gave me a wave and wink in the garden
verb	shows action	gave
direct object	receives action of verb	wave, wink
indirect object	receives object of giving and telling verbs	me
prepositional phrase	a group of words beginning with a preposition and ending with a noun or pronoun	in the garden

101

Case

Nouns and pronouns have different **jobs** to do in a sentence. Here is an example.

John is my friend. He is loyal. I like him. His dog is lost.

He is a subject, *him* is an object, and *his* shows possession. *He, him,* and *his* are different **forms** of the same word. Each **form** has a different **job**.

Form	Job
he	subject
him	object
his	possession

We would not say "Him is loyal" and "I like he." We know without thinking how to use each **form** for the right **job**. **Case** is another word for **job**. Here is the chart above with the case names.

Case	Form	Job
Nominative	he	subject
Objective	him	object
Possessive	his	shows possession

If a word is in the **nominative case**, it has the **job** of being a **subject**. If a word is in the **objective case**, it has the **job** of being an **object**. In Latin there are five cases. Here are the cases and the jobs of each.

Case Name	Job	English
Nominative	subject	
Genitive	possession	's, of
Dative	indirect object	to, for
Accusative	direct object	
Ablative	separation, location, means	in/by/with/from

Notice that the possessive case in English is called the genitive case in Latin; and the objective case in English is called the accusative case in Latin.

Number

In Latin and English grammar, there are two numbers: **singular** and **plural**. **Singular** means *one*; **plural** means *more than one*.

John and Mary are my friends. They are loyal. I like them. Their dog is lost.

They, them, and *their* are the plural forms of *he, him* and *his.* In English we usually add an **s** to make a noun plural: *girl* and *girls.* But some words, such as *man* and *men, child* and *children,* and *he* and *they,* have special forms for the plural.

Declension

Here is a Latin noun listed with all of its case forms in the singular and plural, with an example of the job that each noun is performing. The noun is **rosa**, *rose.*

Case and Number	Form	Possible Meaning	Job
nominative singular	rosa	The rose is red	subject
genitive singular	rosae	scent of the rose, the rose's scent	possession
dative singular	rosae	water for the rose	indirect object
accusative singular	rosam	I picked a rose	direct object
ablative singular	rosā	I got stuck by the rose	means (how)
nominative plural	rosae	The roses grew tall	subject
genitive plural	rosarum	color of roses	quality
dative plural	rosis	talking to the roses	indirect object
accusative plural	rosas	I smell the roses	direct object
ablative plural	rosis	We saw a bee in the roses	location

You will notice that some of the case forms are the same, and that most cases have more than one job. The context of the sentence helps to clarify the precise job of each word.

A **declension** is a table of all the **case forms** of a word, singular and plural. Here is the declension table of the English pronoun *he*.

Case	Singular	Plural	Function
Nominative	he	they	subject
Objective	him	them	object
Possessive	his	their	possession

Writing a noun with all of its forms in a chart is called **declining** a noun. **Incline** goes up and **decline** goes down. The word "decline" comes from the idea of stepping down from the most basic form of a word to the other forms.

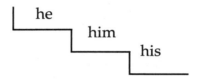

Below is a declension table for the Latin noun **mensa**. It steps down from the dictionary form, **mensa**, through all of the other forms **mensa** can be written in.

First Declension

Case	Singular	Ending	Plural	Ending
Nominative	*mens***a**	-a	*mens***ae**	-ae
Genitive	*mens***ae**	-ae	*mens***arum**	-arum
Dative	*mens***ae**	-ae	*mens***is**	-is
Accusative	*mens***am**	-am	*mens***as**	-as
Ablative	*mens***ā**	-ā	*mens***is**	-is

In Latin there are five families or declensions of nouns. **Mensa** is in the First Declension, and all of the nouns in that declension are declined like **mensa**. All the nouns in a family of nouns have the same or similar endings when they are declined.

Gender

Nouns can be identified as having gender. The words *he, him, his, king, uncle, son,* and *John* are said to be **masculine** because they refer to male persons. The words *she, her, queen, mother, sister,* and *Mary* are said to be **feminine** because they refer to female persons. Words that refer to non-living things, like *rock, table, sun,* and *hope,* have no gender and are said to be **neuter**.

Latin has the **natural** gender, described above, but it also has **grammatical** gender. In **grammatical** gender, non-living things which have no gender are labeled masculine or feminine. Most European languages are like Latin and have grammatical gender: French, German, Spanish, Italian, Russian.

Here are some Spanish words that have grammatical gender:

La Paz   El Paso

La means *the* for a feminine noun. **El** means *the* for a masculine noun. *La Paz* is the capital of Bolivia. *Paz* means peace. *Paz* is feminine even though peace is a thing. It has grammatical gender. *El Paso* is a city in Texas. *Paso* means passage or gateway. *Paso* is a *thing,* but it is masculine in Spanish. *Paz* and *Paso* have grammatical gender.

In Latin, **rosa** is feminine. A rose is a thing, but in Latin it is feminine; it has grammatical gender.

The abbreviations for gender are:

feminine	*f.*
masculine	*m.*
neuter	*n.*

Here are some other nouns in Latin that have grammatical gender. They are all non-living things, but they are identified as masculine or feminine.

mensa	*f.*	*table*		**lux**	*f.*	*light*
mundus	*m.*	*world*		**lacus**	*m.*	*lake*

◆ English and Latin don't have a one-to-one correspondence between their verb tenses. Beginning students should memorize a meaning for each Latin tense. Later they will study them more thoroughly to learn how to translate correctly between the two languages. English often has a verb phrase of 2-4 words that requires only one word in Latin.

◆ English has progressive forms in every tense to show continuous action; Latin does not.

◆ The main difficulty lies in the English past and the Latin perfect and imperfect. Study carefully the second and fourth rows, the English past and present perfect. Notice that the simple past in English, *I called every hour*, requires the imperfect tense in Latin.

English Tenses	Examples	Use in Latin and English	Corresponding Latin Tenses and Examples
Present System			

Present
   Simple
   Progressive
   Emphatic
	I *call* home.
	I *am calling* now.
	I *do call*.
		• General statement
		• Ongoing present action
		• Emphasis
			Present
			      Voco

Past
   Simple
 	
   Progressive
   Emphatic
	I *called* home.
	I *called* every hour.
	I *was calling*.
	I *did call*.
		• Indefinite past time
		• Repeated past action
		• Ongoing past action
		• Emphasis
			Perfect **Vocavi**
			Imperfect **Vocabam**
			Imperfect **Vocabam**
			Perfect **Vocavi**

Future Progressive	I *will call*. I *will be calling*.	• Future action	Future **Vocabo**
Perfect System			
Present Perfect Progressive	I *have called*. I *have been calling* all day.	• Completed action with respect to a present action, or a past action continuing to the present	Perfect **Vocavi** (N.B. The Latin perfect tenses do not have a progressive sense.)

Past Perfect
   Progressive
	I *had called* when you arrived.
	I *had been calling*.
		• Completed action with respect to a past action	Pluperfect
			      Vocáveram

Future Perfect
   Progressive
	I *will have called*.
	I *will have been calling*.
		• A future action completed with respect to another future action	Future Perfect
			      Vocávero

The term "classical pronunciation" refers to modern scholarship's best guess at how Latin may have been pronounced by the educated elite in the late Republic. This guide may be used instead of the Christian pronunciation guide provided in the front of the book.

Vowels

Vowels are either long or short. To keep from cluttering the text, we did not mark each vowel. In practice, it is best to listen to the classical pronunciation audio available from Memoria Press (www.memoriapress.com) to learn the correct vowel sound.

long	as in	example	short	as in	example
ā	*fa*ther	frâter	a*	*a*gain	mensa
ē	*la*te	sêdês	e	*le*t	et
ī	s*ee*n	amîcus	i	s*i*t	cibus
ō	*o*pen	nômen	o	*o*ffer	novem
ū	f*oo*d	lûna	u	f*oo*t	sum

* When short **a** is in a stressed (accented) syllable, it is pronounced like long **ā**.

Diphthongs are long.

Diphthong	as in	example
ae	b*i*te	caelum
oe	b*oi*l	proelium
au	c*ow*	laudo

Consonants

Consonants are pronounced as in English, with the following exceptions:

bs	always pronounced *ps*	urbs
c	always hard: *c*at	voco, cibus
g	always hard: *g*o	fuga, tergi
sc	always hard: e*sc*ape	scribo, discipulus
h	always pronounced *h* except in transliteration of Greek letters (**th**, **ch**, **ph**)	hora, mihi /t-h/: theatrum, /k-h/: chorus, /p-h/: phalanx
qu	as in *qu*it	equus, qui
s	as *s*ing (never as *z*)	mensa, misi
t	as in *t*est	nuntius
v	as *w* in *w*est	verbum (**v** is sometimes written as **u**)

ORAL DRILLS

FOR LESSONS
III, V, IX, X, XIV, XVIII, & XXII

LESSON III

Oral Drill

---

you greet	**1.** salutas	1. they will sail	navigabunt
hsi will overcome	**2.** superabit	2. I was freeing	liberabam
they will walk	**3.** ambulabunt	3. she will judge	judicabit
hsi sets free	**4.** líberat	4. we will walk	ambulábimus
I will judge	**5.** judicabo	5. they look at	spectant
I was adoring	**6.** adorabam	6. I was working	laborabam
you (p) will sail	**7.** navigábitis	7. you will overcome	superabis
hsi was dwelling	**8.** habitabat	8. he will adore	adorabit
we will seize	**9.** occupábimus	9. we are dwelling	habitamus
they were working	**10.** laborabant	10. he greets	salutat

LESSON V

Oral Drill

I will be	**1.** ero	1. they were	erant
you (p) were	**2.** eratis	2. you will be	eris
they will be	**3.** erunt	3. we are	sumus
hsi was	**4.** erat	4. she was	erat
we are	**5.** sumus	5. it will be	erit
we will be	**6.** érimus	6. we were	eramus
you are	**7.** es	7. you (p) will be	éritis
you (p) will be	**8.** éritis	8. it is	est
we were	**9.** eramus	9. I will be	ero
I was	**10.** eram	10. we will be	érimus

LESSON IX

Oral Drill

you had doubted	1. **dubitáveras**	1.	I had hidden	celáveram
we had denied	2. **negaveramus**	2.	she had thought	putáverat
hsi had flown	3. **voláverat**	3.	we had doubted	dubitaveramus
I had thought	4. **putáveram**	4.	they had denied	negáverant
they had hoped	5. **speráverant**	5.	he had asked	rogáverat
hsi had changed	6. **mutáverat**	6.	you (p) had disturbed	perturbaveratis
you (p) had hidden	7. **celaveratis**	7.	you had changed	mutáveras
I had disturbed	8. **perturbáveram**	8.	it had flown	voláverat
you had accused	9. **accusáveras**	9.	they had accused	accusáverant
they had asked	10. **rogáverant**	10.	I had hoped	speráveram

LESSON X

Oral Drill

they w/h reported	1. **nuntiáverint**	1.	I will have wounded	vulnerávero
I w/h explored	2. **explorávero**	2.	you will have explored	exploráveris
you (p) w/h shown	3. **demonstravéritis**	3.	we will have delighted	delectavérimus
you w/h attacked	4. **oppugnáveris**	4.	she will have pointed out	demonstráverit
you (p) w/h created	5. **creavéritis**	5.	they will have created	creáverint
we w/h blamed	6. **culpavérimus**	6.	you (p) will have expected	exspectavéritis
they w/h expected	7. **exspectáverint**	7.	he will have attacked	oppugnáverit
I w/h addressed	8. **appellávero**	8.	we will have blamed	culpavérimus
we w/h wounded	9. **vulneravérimus**	9.	I will have addressed	appellávero
you w/h delighted	10. **delectáveris**	10.	they will have reported	nuntiáverint

LESSON XIV

Oral Drill - Nominative Case

farmers	1. **agrícolae**	1. girl	puella
sailor	2. **nauta**	2. poet	poeta
land	3. **terra**	3. farmer	agrícola
girls	4. **puellae**	4. sailors	nautae
table	5. **mensa**	5. lands	terrae
Italy	6. **Itália**	6. tables	mensae
queens	7. **reginae**	7. Mary	Maria
Mary	8. **Maria**	8. Rome	Roma
Rome	9. **Roma**	9. Italy	Itália
poets	10. **poetae**	10. queen	regina

LESSON XVIII

Oral Drill - Nominative Case

good year	1. **annus bonus**	1. high heaven	altum caelum
new sailors	2. **nautae novi**	2. wide kingdom	latum regnum
bad poet	3. **poeta malus**	3. bad master	dóminus malus
small tables	4. **parvae mensae**	4. large worlds	magni mundi
many gifts	5. **multa dona**	5. small sins	parva débita
large horse	6. **magnus equus**	6. much land	multa terra
eternal friends	7. **amici aeterni**	7. many lands	multae terrae
wide forum	8. **latum forum**	8. new farmer	agrícola novus
high temples	9. **alta templa**	9. holy words	verba sancta
holy queen	10. **regina sancta**	10. good sons	fílii boni

LESSON XXII

Oral Drill - Nominative Case

lights	**1. luces**	1. soldier	miles
bread	**2. panis**	2. soldiers	mílites
sun	**3. sol**	3. feet	pedes
crosses	**4. cruces**	4. sister	soror
soldiers	**5. mílites**	5. cross	crux
soldier	**6. miles**	6. laws	leges
feet	**7. pedes**	7. voices	voces
voice	**8. vox**	8. dogs	canes
leader	**9. dux**	9. sun	sol
foot	**10. pes**	10. customs	mores

VOCABULARY

accuso (1)	to accuse	equus -i m.*	horse
adoro (1)*	to adore	erro (1)	to err, wander
adventus -ūs m.	arrival	exércitus -ūs m.	army
aeternus -a -um*	eternal, everlasting	exploro (1)	to explore
agnus -i m.*	lamb	exspecto (1)	to wait for, expect
agrícola -ae m.	farmer	fácies -ei f.	face
altus -a -um*	high, deep	fides -ei f.	faith, trust
ámbulo (1)*	to walk	fílius -i m.*	son
amicus -i m.*	friend	flumen flúminis n.*	river
amo (1)*	to love, like	forum -i n.*	forum, marketplace
annus -i m.*	year	frater fratris m.*	brother
appáreo (2)	to appear	fructus -ūs m.	fruit
appello (1)*	to address	gáudeo -ēre -- --	to rejoice
árdeo -ēre arsi arsus	to burn, be on fire	hábeo (2)*	to have
aro (1)	to plow	hábito (1)*	to live in, dwell
bellum -i n.*	war	heri	yesterday
bonus -a -um*	good	hódie	today
caelum -i n.*	sky, heaven	Itália -ae f.*	Italy
canis canis m. or f.*	dog	júbeo -ēre jussi jussus*	to order, command
caput cápitis n.*	head	júdico (1)*	to judge, consider
cáveo -ēre cavi cautus	to beware of, guard against	juvo juvare juvi jutus	to help
		laboro (1)*	to work
celo (1)*	to hide	lacus -ūs m.	lake
Christus -i m.*	Christ	latus -a -um	wide, broad
clamo (1)*	to shout	laudo (1)*	to praise
cor cordis n.	heart	lavo lavare lavi lautus*	to wash
cras	tomorrow	lex legis f.*	law
creo (1)	to create	líbero (1)*	to set free
crux crucis f.*	cross	lumen lúminis n.	lamp
culpo (1)	to blame	lux lucis f.*	light
débeo (2)*	to owe, ought	magnus -a -um*	great, large
débitum -i n.*	debt, sin	malus -a -um*	bad
decem*	ten	máneo -ēre mansi mansus	to remain, stay
décimus -a -um	tenth	manus -ūs f.	hand
delecto (1)	to delight, please	Maria -ae f.*	Mary
demonstro (1)	to show, point out	mater matris f.*	mother
deus -i m.*	god	mensa -ae f.*	table
dies -ei m.	day	metus -ūs m.	fear
do dare dedi datus*	to give	miles mílitis m.*	soldier
dóceo -ēre dócui doctus*	to teach	móneo (2)*	to warn
dóminus -i m.*	lord, master	mos moris m.	custom
domus -ūs f.	house, home	móveo -ēre movi motus*	to move
donum -i n.*	gift	multus -a -um*	much, many
dúbito (1)	to doubt	mundus -i m.*	world, mankind
duo*	two	muto (1)	to change
dux ducis m.	leader	narro (1)*	to tell

nato (1)	to swim	Roma -ae f.*	Rome
nauta -ae m.*	sailor	saepe*	often
návigo (1)*	to sail	saluto (1)	to greet
nego (1)	to deny	sanctus -a -um*	sacred, holy
nomen nóminis n.*	name	saxum -i n.	rock
non*	not	secundus -a -um*	second
nonus -a -um	ninth	sédeo -ēre sedi sessus*	to sit
novem*	nine	semper*	always
novus -a -um*	new	senatus -ūs m.	senate
numquam*	never	septem*	seven
nunc*	now	séptimus -a -um	seventh
núntio (1)	to report	servo (1)	to guard, keep
óccupo (1)*	to seize	servus -i m.*	slave, servant
octavus -a -um	eighth	sex*	six
octo*	eight	sextus -a -um	sixth
óppidum -i n.*	town	sol solis m.	sun
oppugno (1)	to attack	soror sororis f.*	sister
opto (1)	to desire, wish	specto (1)*	to look at
oro (1)*	to speak, pray	spero (1)	to hope
panis panis m.	bread	spes -ei f.	hope
paro (1) *	to prepare	spíritus -ūs m.	spirit
parvus -a -um*	small	sto stare steti status	to stand
pater patris m.*	father	sum esse fui futurus	to be
pax pacis f.*	peace	súpero (1)*	to overcome, surpass
perturbo (1)	to disturb	táceo (2)	to be silent
pes pedis m.	foot	templum -i n.	temple
poeta -ae m.	poet	tempto (1)	to tempt
porto (1)*	to carry	téneo -ēre ténui tentus	to hold
portus -ūs m.	harbor	terra -ae f.*	earth, land
primus -a -um*	first	térreo (2)*	to frighten
prohíbeo (2)	to prevent	tértius -a -um*	third
puella -ae f.*	girl	tímeo -ēre tímui --*	to fear, be afraid of
pugno (1)*	to fight	tres*	three
puto (1)	to think	tum	then, at that time
quartus -a -um	fourth	umquam	ever
quáttuor*	four	unus -a -um*	one
quinque*	five	váleo -ēre válui --	to be strong, be well
quintus -a -um	fifth	*verbum -i n.*	word
regina -ae f.*	queen	vídeo -ēre vidi visus*	to see
regnum -i n.*	kingdom	voco (1)*	to call
res -ei f.	thing, matter, affair, business	volo (1)	to fly
		vox vocis f.*	voice
respóndeo -ēre respondi responsus	to respond, answer	vúlnero (1)	to wound
rex regis m.*	king	
rogo (1)	to ask	

*Vocabulary included in *Latina Christiana*, *4th Edition*

117

accuse	accuso (1)	earth	terra -ae f.
address	appello (1)	eight	octo
adore	adoro (1)	eighth	octavus -a -um
affair	res -ei f.	err	erro (1)
always	semper	eternal	aeternus -a -um
answer	respondeo ēre respondi	ever	umquam
	responsus	everlasting	aeternus -a -um
appear	appáreo (2)	expect	exspecto (1)
army	exércitus -ūs m.	explore	exploro (1)
arrival	adventus -ūs m.	face	fácies -ei f.
ask	rogo (1)	faith	fides -ei f.
attack	oppugno (1)	farmer	agrícola -ae m.
at that time	tum	father	pater patris m.
bad	malus -a -um	fear (noun)	metus -ūs m.
be	sum esse fui futurus	fear (verb)	tímeo -ēre timui --
be afraid of	tímeo -ēre tímui --	fifth	quintus -a -um
be on fire	árdeo -ēre arsi arsus	fight	pugno (1)
be silent	táceo (2)	first	primus -a -um
be strong	váleo -ēre válui --	five	quinque
be well	váleo -ēre válui --	fly	volo (1)
beware of	cáveo -ēre cavi cautus	foot	pes pedis m.
blame	culpo (1)	forum	forum -i n.
bread	panis panis m.	four	quáttuor
broad	latus -a -um	fourth	quartus -a -um
brother	frater fratris m.	friend	amicus -i m.
burn	árdeo -ēre arsi arsus	frighten	térreo (2)
business	res -ei f.	fruit	fructus -ūs m.
call	voco (1)	gift	donum -i n.
carry	porto (1)	girl	puella -ae f.
change	muto (1)	give	do dare dedi datus
Christ	Christus -i m.	god	deus -i m.
command	júbeo -ēre jussi jussus	good	bonus -a -um
consider	júdico (1)	great	magnus -a -um
create	creo (1)	greet	saluto (1)
cross	crux crucis f.	guard	servo (1)
custom	mos moris m.	guard against	cáveo -ēre cavi cautus
day	dies -ei m.	hand	manus -ūs f.
debt	débitum -i n.	harbor	portus -ūs m.
deep	altus -a -um	have	hábeo (2)
delight	delecto (1)	head	caput cápitis n.
deny	nego (1)	heart	cor cordis n.
desire	opto (1)	heaven	caelum -i n.
disturb	perturbo (1)	help	juvo juvare juvi jutus
dog	canis canis m. or f.	hide	celo (1)
doubt	dúbito (1)	high	altus -a -um
dwell	hábito (1)	hold	téneo -ēre ténui tentus

holy	**sanctus -a -um**	peace	**pax pacis f.**
home	**domus -ūs f.**	please	**delecto (1)**
hope (noun)	**spes -ei f.**	plow	**aro (1)**
hope (verb)	**spero (1)**	poet	**poeta -ae m.**
horse	**equus -i m.**	point out	**demonstro (1)**
house	**domus -ūs f.**	praise	**laudo (1)**
Italy	**Itália -ae f.**	pray	**oro (1)**
judge	**júdico (1)**	prepare	**paro (1)**
keep	**servo (1)**	prevent	**prohíbeo (2)**
king	**rex regis m.**	queen	**regina -ae f.**
kingdom	**regnum -i n.**	rejoice	**gáudeo -ēre -- --**
lake	**lacus -ūs m.**	remain	**máneo -ēre mansi mansus**
lamb	**agnus -i m.**	report	**núntio (1)**
lamp	**lumen lúminis n.**	respond	**respóndeo -ēre respondi**
land	**terra -ae f.**		**responsus**
large	**magnus -a -um**	river	**flumen flúminis n.**
law	**lex legis f.**	rock	**saxum -i n.**
leader	**dux ducis m.**	Rome	**Roma -ae f.**
light	**lux lucis f.**	sacred	**sanctus -a -um**
like	**amo (1)**	sail	**návigo (1)**
live in	**hábito (1)**	sailor	**nauta -ae m.**
look at	**specto (1)**	second	**secundus -a -um**
lord	**dóminus -i m.**	see	**vídeo -ēre vidi visus**
love	**amo (1)**	seize	**óccupo (1)**
mankind	**mundus -i m.**	senate	**senatus -ūs m.**
many	**multi -ae -a** *(plural)*	servant	**servus -i m.**
marketplace	**forum -i n.**	set free	**líbero (1)**
Mary	**Maria -ae f.**	seven	**septem**
master	**dóminus -i m.**	seventh	**séptimus -a -um**
matter	**res -ei f.**	shout	**clamo (1)**
mother	**mater matris f.**	show	**demonstro (1)**
move	**móveo -ēre movi motus**	sin	**débitum -i n.**
much	**multus -a -um** *(sing)*	sister	**soror sororis f.**
name	**nomen nóminis n.**	sit	**sédeo -ēre sedi sessus**
never	**numquam**	six	**sex**
new	**novus -a -um**	sixth	**sextus -a -um**
nine	**novem**	sky	**caelum -i n.**
ninth	**nonus -a -um**	slave	**servus -i m.**
not	**non**	small	**parvus -a -um**
now	**nunc**	soldier	**miles mílitis m.**
often	**saepe**	son	**fílius -i m.**
one	**unus -a -um**	speak	**oro (1)**
order	**júbeo -ēre jussi jussus**	spirit	**spíritus -ūs m.**
ought	**débeo (2)**	stand	**sto stare steti status**
overcome	**súpero (1)**	stay	**máneo -ēre mansi mansus**
owe	**débeo (2)**	sun	**sol solis m.**

surpass	**súpero (1)**
swim	**nato (1)**
table	**mensa -ae f.**
teach	**dóceo -ēre dócui doctus**
tell	**narro (1)**
temple	**templum -i n.**
tempt	**tempto (1)**
ten	**decem**
tenth	**décimus -a -um**
then	**tum**
thing	**res -ei f.**
think	**puto (1)**
third	**tértius -a -um**
three	**tres**
today	**hódie**
tomorrow	**cras**
town	**óppidum -i n.**
trust	**fides -ei f.**
two	**duo**
voice	**vox vocis f.**
wait for	**exspecto (1)**
walk	**ámbulo (1)**
wander	**erro (1)**
war	**bellum -i n.**
warn	**móneo (2)**
wash	**lavo lavare lavi lautus**
wide	**latus -a -um**
wish	**opto (1)**
word	**verbum -i n.**
work	**laboro (1)**
world	**mundus -i m.**
wound	**vúlnero (1)**
year	**annus -i m.**
yesterday	**heri**

¹ In this course, long vowels are marked only to distinguish certain grammatical forms, such as the ablative singular ending in the first declension (**mensā**), the infinitive of the second conjugation (**monēre**), and the genitive singular, nominative and accusative plural of the fourth declension (**portūs**).

² The present stem is derived from the infinitive; Lesson IV has a fuller treatment of the present stem.

³ The 4th principal part can be written with the ending **um** or **us**. This text uses **us** because that is consistent with the dictionary form for adjectives and the 4th principal part is a participle (verbal adjective). The Henle text uses **us** for transitive verbs and **um** for intransitive verbs, but this text is not making that distinction at this point.

⁴ The general rule for finding the stem of Latin nouns is to "drop the ending of the genitive singular." This rule will be given in lesson XXI when students can see the reason for it.

⁵ The nominative singular ending is a short vowel and the ablative singular ending is long. The use of the macron here is to help students recognize the different cases in writing, not to make a pronunciation distinction between long and short vowels, which we are not emphasizing in this text.

⁶ **Caelum** is masculine in the plural: **caeli -orum**.

⁷ Forms of **unus** and **tres** will be used in cases where they are regular.

⁸ The 3rd declension also has **i-stem** nouns which will be covered in *Second Form*.